Collins discover

Opera

Clive Griffin

Collins

An Imprint of HarperCollins*Publishers*

ISBN-13: 978-0-00-724145-3
ISBN-10: 0-00-724145-3

ISBN: 978-0-06-124182-6 (in the United States)
ISBN-10: 0-06-124182-2
FIRST U.S. EDITION. Published in 2007.

Created by **Focus Publishing**, Sevenoaks, Kent
Project editor: Guy Croton
Designer: Diarmuid Moloney
Series design: Mark Thomson

Color reproduction by Colourscan, Singapore
Printed and bound by Printing Express Ltd.

11 10 09 08 07
6 5 4 3 2 1

Contents

Introduction

This book is for those of you who have perhaps heard, and enjoyed, operatic extracts. You want to know more but do not know quite where to start. Hopefully, the following chapters will give you the knowledge and confidence to explore farther.

The popular quartet Il Divo has brought opera to an alternative and much wider international audience in recent years.

Seeing the whole picture

In many ways, opera has never had a wider audience. The success of the Four Tenors' concerts, the popularity of groups such as Il Divo and Opera Babes, the expansion of classical music radio stations in Europe, and the increasing use of operatic extracts in movies and commercials have all served to bring an awareness of the beauty and emotional power of opera to those who have never set foot inside an opera house. The emphasis in all of the above, however, is on excerpts. To enjoy a single aria or chorus from an opera without hearing, and seeing, a complete performance is like admiring a single rose without ever visiting a rose garden or watching trailers without ever seeing a complete movie.

What is opera?

An opera is a drama in which all or part of the dialog is sung rather than spoken and which also contains instrumental interludes. Put very simply, drama appeals to our intellect through words while music appeals to our feelings. It is through the combination of these two elements that opera gains its unique power to move us. The music in an opera is not merely an accompaniment to the words: it serves to comment on the drama and to heighten the emotion. A successful opera performance relies on the creative partnership between the conductor, the stage designer, the stage director, and, of course, the singers and orchestra.

Operetta and musicals

Opera generally deals with universal themes of life and death, heroism, and betrayal. Operetta, literally "small opera," is generally more lighthearted in nature and often humorous. It often has a distinctly national character, ranging from the French operettas of Jacques Offenbach to the German ones of Franz Lehár and the unmistakably British compositions of Gilbert and Sullivan.

In the United States, operetta was combined with elements of vaudeville, minstrel shows, and jazz to create the musical comedy, or musical. In musicals, songs and choruses, elaborate dance routines, and instrumental interludes are integrated into a dramatic plot, often with a contemporary setting.

The tenor Arnold Rawls in the title role of the late 19th century Italian *verismo* opera *Pagliacci*, by Leoncavallo.

How to use this book

The main focus of this book is on the way that opera has developed from its earliest beginnings to the present day. This will help you to put operatic works into their historical and musical context. There are brief introductions to the major composers of opera and their contributions to its development. A chapter at the end of the book comprises a section dealing with the actual staging of opera. Finally, interspersed throughout the book there are brief synopses of the plots of eleven operas, each representative of a different stage in opera's development. Rather than a discography, a selection of recommended DVD performances of operas has been provided at the close of the book.

1 In the beginning

It is generally agreed that the first opera was *Dafne*, written in Florence in 1597 by Jacopo Peri. This work did not suddenly appear from nowhere, however, and to understand the roots of opera we have to go all the way back to ancient Greek theater. We also need to consider Medieval musical dramas and Renaissance court spectacles involving pageantry, music, and dance, such as the masque and the intermedio.

The roots of opera

The theater of ancient Greece was an arena in which stories such as those of Electra, Oedipus, or Orpheus and Eurydice (see page 8) set out to explore moral issues and to remind the audience of the consequences of human actions.

The ancient Greek tale of Orpheus and Eurydice laid down story-telling conventions that feature in opera and related musical forms to this day.

Ancient Greek theater

A feature of ancient Greek theater was the chorus, which served as a kind of teacher to the audience and made moral comments on the action that was played out before it. The verses written for the chorus were set to music. Speeches by individual characters were possibly also sung and instrumental music was played during certain passages of the play. The ancient Greeks appreciated that, on a practical level, words carry farther when sung than when spoken. On an artistic level, music can serve to emphasize the abstract and emotional elements of a play. Roman theater drew on this Greek model, especially the inclusion of music, laying the foundations for the later development of opera in Italy.

The Middle Ages

Although the religious dramas of the Middle Ages (the Mystery Plays) often had a musical element, it is within the secular music dramas of this period that the roots of opera can be found. It is also at this time that we can finally put a name to a composer. *Le Jeu de Robin et de Marion* by Adam de la Halle, first performed in Naples in 1282, is a pastoral comedy that combines song, speech, and dance. It is widely recognized as a significant forerunner of opera.

Adam de la Halle

Adam de la Halle was born sometime around 1240. As a boy, he studied grammar, theology, and music at the Cistercian Abbey of Vaucelles. He had been destined for the church, but renounced this intention and married a girl named Marie, who figures in many of his songs. Later, he joined the household of Robert II, Count of Artois, and then was attached to Charles of Anjou. It was at the court of Charles, who had become king of Naples, that he wrote his *Le Jeu de Robin et de Marion*, the most famous of his works. It is cited as the earliest French play with music to be based upon a secular subject. It consists of dialog interspersed with melodies that were already current in popular folk music.

The Renaissance

The term *renaissance* (rebirth) refers to that period in European history which divides the Middle Ages from modern times. It was a time when there was a new and wider interest in the arts and learning. The Renaissance began in Italy in the 14th century, particularly in Florence, and spread throughout the rest of Europe during the following two hundred years. Historians are divided as to what actually triggered the Renaissance, but one theory is that the fall of Constantinople to the Muslims in 1453 led to an influx of Byzantine-Greek scholars into Italy. This led to a renewed interest into Europe's Greek and Roman heritage. It was during this period that the influence of the Church over music began to wane, as composers were also able to find aristocratic patrons who were anxious to lavish money on musical and

Decorative masks have been used in opera and its antecedents for centuries.

dramatic entertainments that displayed their wealth and prestige. Two such aristocratic art forms were direct forerunners of opera.

Masquerade

The masquerade (or masque) was a form of festive courtly entertainment in which those taking part hid their faces with masks. (A public version of the masque was the pageant.) Masque, which was born in Italy, involved music and dancing, singing, and acting. Masques employed elaborate stage designs, often by a well-known architect. Professional actors and musicians were hired for the speech and song aspects, while the other parts would be played by courtiers.

Intermedio

The intermedio was a play with musical interludes written for special occasions. Intermedi were often performed at aristocratic weddings and state occasions. Often the subject matter of the intermedio was a mythological story, which could be told in mime or by dance. Another popular favorite was the pastorale, which presented an idealized view of nature.

OPPOSITE: **A painting entitled "Elegant Company Preparing for a Masked Ball," by Luis Paret y Alcázar.**

The Camerata

In late 16th century Florence, a group known as the Camerata Fiorentina (or Florence Academy) was born. It consisted of poets and musicians who rejected the music and drama of their day. They took their inspiration from what they saw as the purity of ancient Greece and based much of their work on myths and tragedies.

must know

Jacopo Peri (1561–1633) is often called the inventor of opera. In the 1590s, Peri became associated with Jacopo Corsi, the leading patron of music in Florence. Believing that contemporary art was inferior to classical Greek and Roman works, they decided to attempt to recreate Greek tragedy as they understood it, though today their efforts are thought to be a long way from anything the Greeks would have recognized. Although their second collaboration, *Eurydice*, has survived to the present day, it is rarely staged.

Monody

The importance of the Camerata to the development of opera was that they believed that words and music should serve each other, but that the words should always be understood. They felt that vocal music should follow the inflections and rhythms of spoken text rather than the regular beat of dance tunes. Furthermore, they thought that it should illustrate the emotions inherent in the words. They developed a form of vocal music called monody (from the Greek for "solo song"). The accompaniment consisted of a series of chords on a harpsichord, supported by a bass melody instrument. (This is referred to as basso continuo.)

The first opera

Two members of the Camerata, Giulio Caccini and Jacopo Peri, set out to create dramatic works based on these theories, using monody for dialog and soliloquies. In 1597, Peri wrote what is generally accepted to be the first opera, *Dafne*. In 1600, he composed *Eurydice*, the first opera to survive with its music complete.

The story of Orpheus and Eurydice has been a subject for opera since its very beginning. The mythical figure of Orpheus was seen as the chief

A contemporary production of
Jacopo Peri's *Dafne*, which is
rarely performed nowadays.

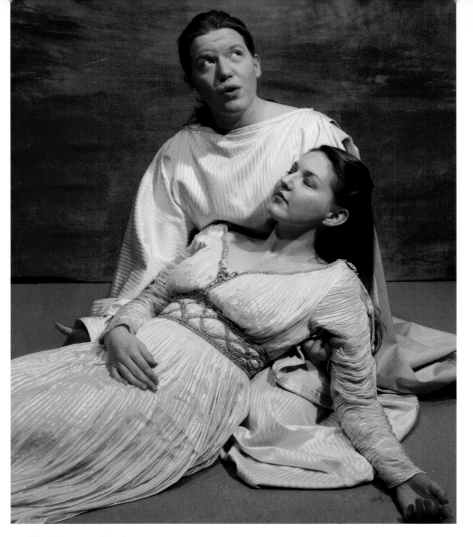

Jennifer Johnson and Barbara Dineen in a scene from a rare modern production of *Orpheus and Eurydice*, staged by Webster University in 2006.

poet and musician of antiquity. His mother was Calliope, the Muse of poetry, and he was taught music by the god Apollo. With his music and singing, he could calm wild beasts and even control the forces of nature. When his wife, Eurydice, died, Orpheus went down to the lower world and, with his music, softened the heart of the god Hades, who agreed to allow Eurydice to return to earth. A condition attached was that he should walk in front of her and not turn around until he had reached the upper world. Unfortunately, he could not resist looking back and she vanished from his sight.

Jacopo Peri's operatic version of the famous old story was written for the celebration of the wedding of Maria de 'Medici to the French King Henri IV. It is unusual in that it gives the tale a happy ending, presumably not to depress the wedding guests. Additional elements to the score were provided by Giulio Caccini, whose own version of *Eurydice*, published before Peri's, was performed in Florence two years later.

So why don't we hear them today?

The works created by members of the Camerata, although vital to the development of opera, were rather staid and academic. What they lacked was passion and human interest. Their composers were more concerned with demonstrating theories than creating characters and stirring the emotions. If performed at all nowadays, their works are staged for their historical interest. What the new art form needed was a genius who could breathe life into it, and the first genius of opera was Claudio Monteverdi.

2 Early Italian opera

During the Renaissance, Italy was a collection of city-states, each with its own ruler—the Pope in Rome, the Medici family in Florence, the Doge in Venice, and so on. There was constant, often violent, rivalry amongst the ruling families of these city states, which led to economic and artistic competition to achieve the most brilliant court. Opera provided a perfect vehicle for the expression of this rivalry, due to its ideal disposition for the conspicuous display of wealth and patronage.

Monteverdi

The first composer to create opera that can still move a modern audience was Claudio Monteverdi. He understood that opera must be based on more than academic theory. It had to live and breathe if it was to stir the emotions and capture the imagination.

Monteverdi's early years

Monteverdi was baptized on May 15th, 1567 in Cremona, northern Italy. During his long career, he produced works that marked the transition from Renaissance to Baroque music. He wrote his first music for publication as early as 1582 and shortly after he had completed his first book of secular madrigals, in 1587, he began to look for work outside of his native town.

Monteverdi's first opera, *Orfeo*, was staged at the court of Mantua in 1607. This was followed by a second, *Arianna*, commissioned for the wedding of Francesco di Gonzaga to Marguerite of Savoy. Monteverdi's wife fell ill and died while he was working on this opera, and it is said that he poured his grief into the music. Only a fragment of the opera survives, the aria "Lamento di Arianna," which is still a popular concert item today.

Monteverdi's contribution to opera

Monteverdi's operas developed the use of singing forms that remain an integral part of opera today, the recitative, the aria, the arioso, and the chorus. Monteverdi was probably the first composer to assign specific instruments to parts. Each instrument was used not only to create orchestral

Probably the most dominant force in early Italian opera, Monteverdi had a huge influence on the work of his contemporaries.

Monteverdi's operas were groundbreaking not only because they were imbued with drama and passion but also because of the subjects they dealt with. This is a scene from *L'Incoronazione di Poppea*.

color, but also to describe characters. In his opera *Orfeo*, for example, Orpheus is usually accompanied by a harp, the shepherds by flutes, and the gods of the underworld by trombones.

Later life

In 1613, Monteverdi moved to Venice, where he took up the post of *maestro di cappella* (head of music) of the Church of San Marco. He became a priest and devoted himself to the composition of religious music, but he also continued to write operas, only two of which survive. Of these, *L'Incoronazione di Poppea* is notable for being based on an historical rather than a mythological subject. Monteverdi's successors went on to create further operas with real people as their subject, thus opening the way for new themes and styles. Monteverdi himself died in 1643.

must know

- Recitativo—also referred to as recitative in English—is a form of singing that follows the rhythms of speech (think of the word reciting). It is used to move on the action in operas.
- Aria (from the Italian word for air) was originally any expressive melody, but it came to be used to refer to a self-contained piece for one voice usually with orchestral accompaniment.
- Chorus—The word chorus in opera refers to both the ensemble of singers who perform the non-soloist parts of an opera and to the actual music that they sing.

Different cities, different styles

The popularity of opera quickly spread to other Italian cities. Different styles developed in each, but, as composers often moved from one to another in search of patrons, there was also much sharing of ideas.

A poster advertising Benedetto Ferrari's *L'Andromeda*, performed in Venice in 1637.

Venice

With the opening of the Teatro San Cassiano in 1637, opera became a popular form of entertainment with the merchants and professional classes as well as the aristocracy. Sixteen further theaters were opened and, by 1700, nearly four hundred operas had been staged. The Venetians had a penchant for spectacular visual effects and lavish staging. Among composers of such spectacular operas, the most notable was Antonio Cesti.

Antonio Cesti (1623–69) was born in Tuscany but worked in Florence, Rome, and Venice. He also traveled to Vienna, introducing Italian opera to the German-speaking world. The most celebrated of Cesti's operas was *Il Pomo d'oro* (*The Golden Apple*), performed for the wedding of the Holy Roman Emperor, Leopold I, and Margaret Theresa, daughter of Philip IV of Spain, in 1666. The elaborate staging of this opera employed various mechanical devices to provide such spectacles as gods descending from heaven, naval battles, and storms. Cesti also contributed to the development of opera through his use of large choruses for dramatic emphasis and by stressing the importance of vocal ornamentation in his arias. Coloratura signifies the decoration of a vocal melody in the shape of runs, roulades, and cadenzas.

An idealized mural painting of Venice in the 17th century, based on views of the city by Canaletto.

Historically Rome had always set itself apart from the rest of Italy, and the same could be said of the city's approach to early opera.

Rome

Roman opera differed from other Italian forms in that it focused more on religious subjects than on Greek mythology. The chorus in Roman opera also had a more important role and was used more extensively. The aria and the recitativo were beginning to become more distinct and greatly differed from one another. The intermezzi, which were originally light interludes between acts of an opera, provided a model for what was later to become the comedic opera style.

Naples

Naples was the second great city of Italian opera after Venice. Composers associated with the city included Alessandro Scarlatti (1660–1725, pictured on page 18), Arcangelo Corelli (1653–1713), and Giovanni Pergolesi (1710–1736). These composers embraced all the styles that had been created from the beginning of the 17th century, experimenting with melody, orchestration, and the blending of comic and tragic elements. Perhaps their most important contribution to the development of opera, however, was that many Neapolitan musicians traveled throughout Europe, taking this new art form with them.

Neapolitan opera is often known as *opera seria*—or "serious opera"—due to the themes that Scarlatti and his contemporaries explored in their work. The primary musical emphasis of opera seria was on the solo voice and on *bel canto*, the very florid vocal style of the period (see pages 82–3).

A portrait of King Ferdinand IV of Naples, aged nine. The king ruled the city as its own distinctive form of opera began to flourish.

The Castrati

A feature of early Italian opera was the popularity of the Castrati, who gave up so much in the cause of music. As the name suggests, they were male singers who had been castrated in order to prevent their voices from breaking at puberty.

must know

Da capo arias—the name given to a form of aria following an A-B-A scheme, in which the singer performed improvized variations when the A section was repeated. The term *da capo* translates as "from the beginning."

Who were the Castrati?

The practice of castration of singers began in the 16th century. The Roman Catholic Church banned females from singing in church, but as somebody was needed to sing the top line in choir music, castration provided a solution. The Castrati were selected as boy singers, either orphans or from poor families who hoped for later financial reward. By 1640, Castrati were in use in church choirs throughout Italy and were beginning to make their appearance on the opera stage. Although

The most famous of all the Castrati, Farinelli. His real name was Carlo Broschi and he lived in Italy from 1705 to 1782.

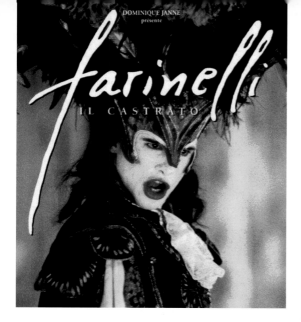

A modern-day DVD cover for a recent French movie about the life and times of Farinelli, directed by Gérard Corbiau.

the operation, performed on boys between the ages of four and seven, was illegal, more than 4,000 boys were castrated in Italy during the 18th century.

The first opera superstars

The Castrati were highly thought of and, pampered and over-indulged, were the first popular music stars. They were particularly idolized by women. They retained youthful voices into old age but suffered physically. Most were fat, with huge chests (or even breasts) but thin arms and legs. They were valued for their vocal ability rather than their acting skills. Their main claim to fame was their incredible breath control, the ability to execute complicated passages without any obvious strain, and a vocal range of three octaves. With the popularity of the Castrati, however, operas came to consist of little more than a series of spectacular arias. The last castrato was Alessandro Moreschi, who died in 1922. His voice was actually captured on a few early gramophone records.

want to know more?

The following books will give you more information about the Renaissance in Italy:
- *The Italian Renaissance: Culture and Society in Italy* by Peter Burke (Polity Press, 1999)
- *The Italian Renaissance* by J.H.Plumb (Mariner Books, 2001)

3 Opera in France and England

18th century composers had to be prepared to travel if they wanted to find patrons and this often meant relocating to another country. Thus it is that the French school of opera was founded by an Italian, Giovanni Battista Lulli, while the most popular composer in England was a German, Georg Friedrich Händel. They are, of course, better known by the names they used in their adoptive countries, Jean-Baptiste Lully and George Frideric Handel.

Opera in France

Lully's patron was Louis XIV, the "Sun King," and his operas, with their stately choral and instrumental episodes, reflect the pageantry and splendor of Versailles. In keeping with royal tastes, the operas also included extended dance sequences and were based on stories that lent themselves to great spectacle.

Jean Baptiste Lully made a crucial contribution to the evolution of opera and established a unique style of his own in the process.

Jean Baptiste Lully

Despite being an Italian, Lully established the traditions that became hallmarks of French opera and which differentiated it from the Italian style that had become dominant elsewhere in Europe. Lully's life was certainly interesting. Born Giovanni Battista Lulli in Florence on November 28th, 1632, he was the son of a miller, though he later claimed that his father was a nobleman. He had little musical education but had a natural talent for playing the guitar and dancing. In 1646, he was "discovered" by the Duke of Guise, who took him to France, where he found work as a kitchen hand. His employer, Mademoiselle de Montpensier, was obviously taken with him and provided a teacher to cultivate his musical talents. However, unfortunately she discovered an obscene poem which he had written about her and he was dismissed.

At the court of the Sun King

By 1653, Lully was a dancer at the court of Louis XIV. He composed some ballet music, which the king liked, and was appointed as the court orchestral composer. As the king became older and lost his enthusiasm (and ability) for dancing, Lully, who had

It was the patronage of the most powerful monarch in Europe – Louis XIV, the Sun King – that enabled Lully to flourish.

become a French citizen in 1661, turned to writing opera instead. He exercised iron control over the musical life at court, supervising all orchestral and choral rehearsals. In 1687, while beating out time during a rehearsal, he drove the pole he was using through his foot and died of the resultant gangrene.

Lully's contribution to opera

Lully's most important contribution to the development of opera in France was his emphasis on the clear enunciation of words. His works were referred to as *tragédie-lyrique* and were very much plays set to music. The libretti (texts) of his operas were based on classical French tragedy and their melodic lines follow the

The Palais de Versailles—the hub of Louis XIV's extensive empire and home to Lully for much of his adult life.

rhythms and inflections of the French language. The arioso style, although developed in Italy, came to have more influence in France. Lully's other great contribution was his establishment of a standardized overture form, the French overture.

The overture

The first operas had no overture, but were introduced by singers, who summarized the action to follow in a vocal prolog. Monteverdi's *Orfeo* had an instrumental introduction, but the notion of a standardized overture begins with Lully. He devised a scheme which, although he himself did not always adhere to it, consists of a slow introduction in a marked "dotted rhythm," followed by a lively movement in fugato style. The slow introduction was always repeated. The operatic French overture was often followed by a suite of dance tunes before the curtain finally rose.

must know

The *arioso* is a cross between a *recitativo* and an *aria*. Usually accompanied by a full orchestra, it is more melodic than a *recitativo accompagnato*.

French opera after Lully

Jean-Philippe Rameau (1683–1764) was a student of Lully. He was a noted musical theorist and published a number of works on composition and performance. His first opera, *Hippolyte et Aricie*, was not written until 1733, followed by *Les Indes Galantes* in 1735 and *Castor et Pollux* in 1737. His early operas led to dispute between those who favored the style of Lully and those who felt that French opera should move on. Rameau felt that the works of Lully had placed too much emphasis on spectacle and he sought to strike more of a balance between the different elements of opera. Rameau's operas were greatly admired by later French composers such as Berlioz and Debussy.

must know

Some musical terms:
- Overture—an instrumental introduction to an opera (or ballet).
- Fugato—a piece of music written in the style of a fugue without following the rules strictly.
- Fugue—a piece of music which begins with a theme stated by one of the voices playing alone. A second voice then enters and plays the same theme, while the first voice continues on with a contrapuntal accompaniment. The remaining voices enter one by one, each beginning by stating the same theme.

Jean-Philippe Rameau studied under Lully and followed his lead after his mentor's death as a result of a freak accident in 1687.

Opera in England

In the 18th century the London theater remained a popular form of entertainment once the playhouses reopened following the Restoration. Music had become an increasingly common component of theatrical performances and it was from this tradition that the first English opera, Henry Purcell's *Dido and Aeneas*, was born.

Henry Purcell

Born in Westminster in 1659, Henry Purcell (pictured both on page 28 and opposite) was a chorister in the Chapel Royal until his voice broke in 1673. In 1679 he succeeded his teacher, John Blow, as organist of Westminster Abbey. From that time he began writing music for the theater as well as for royal occasions. He died in 1695. According to legend, he caught a fatal chill when his wife locked him out after he returned home late from the theater.

Purcell's contribution to English opera

Purcell's greatest talent was for setting the English language to music. This talent has been an inspiration to such 20th century British composers as Benjamin Britten and Michael Tippett. He composed settings of the works of such writers as Dryden, Congreve, and Behn. His opera *Dido and Aeneas*, produced between 1688 and 1690, is generally regarded as the first English opera. There is no spoken dialog, but instead the action progresses in recitatives. It was probably composed for a private performance at Josias Priest's boarding school for young gentlewomen and all the roles, male and female, were sung by girls. The opera appears to have

Henry Purcell could rightfully lay claim to being the father of English opera, although some of his most famous work was not properly staged until long after his death.

been very popular at private performances but its wider theatrical possibilities were not recognized during Purcell's lifetime. It was not finally staged until 1895, two hundred years after his death.

The semi-operas

Purcell also composed four other works which can best be described as semi-operas. *The Fairy Queen* (loosely based on Shakespeare's *A Midsummer Night's Dream*), *Dioclesian*, *The Indian Queen*, and *King Arthur* were spectacles that were a development of earlier court entertainments known as masques. They included dialog, dance, orchestral music, and songs.

must know

Josias (or Josiah) Priest (1645–1735) was an English dancing teacher and choreographer. In 1675 he opened his first boarding school for young gentlewomen, followed by a second one in 1680. Here he hosted performances of operas by Purcell and John Blow. He possibly also choreographed dances for these operas.

Handel

By far the most successful composer of opera in 18th century London was George Frideric Handel. His career is a useful example of the fact that the production of opera in the 18th century was as much a business venture as an artistic one.

George Frideric Handel in later life.

Handel's early life

Handel, who was born in Saxony in 1685, started his career as a church organist. He was attracted to the theater, however, and in 1703 he moved to Hamburg, where the first public opera house outside Italy had been opened in 1678. He moved to Italy in 1706, where he became a very popular composer of operas, generally drawing upon mythological subjects or stories of Greek and Roman heroes. His greatest success was with the opera *Agrippina*, which was first performed in Venice in 1707. In 1710, he took up a position as court musician to the Elector of Hanover. Later the same year, he was granted permission to visit England. The political situation there was different to that in other parts of Europe. The absolute power of the monarchy had been broken and there was an emerging middle class, anxious to display its culture and breeding by offering patronage to composers and artists. Handel's music enjoyed popular success and he returned in 1712. Although this was only meant to be a temporary stay, he decided to settle in London.

must know

The notion of the composer as an artist is a relatively recent one. In earlier centuries, they were seen as skilled craftsmen supplying music for particular occasions or patrons. It was possible to earn a living from music, but composers needed either employment from the Church or in royal courts, or the support of rich patrons. Handel was one of the first composers to break away from this system.

Entrepreneur and composer

In 1714, Queen Anne of England, who had granted Handel a pension of £200 a year, died. Her successor was George, Elector of Hanover, the employer from whom Handel had been absent for over two years. Handel made his peace with his former employer, however, and was granted a pension of £400 a year, with an additional £200 from the Princess of Wales. Using this money, in addition to financial backing from members of the English nobility, Handel launched his own opera company. In the 1720s this venture went bankrupt, but Handel had done so well that he was able to put the enormous sum of £10,000 into a new company. This new venture also folded in 1737. Destructive rivalries and poor management were part of the problem, but probably the main reason for their failure was a simple change in public taste. The huge success of John Gay's *The Beggar's Opera*, a satirical work sung in English, had turned London audiences away from Italian opera.

The later years

After the collapse of his opera ventures, Handel concentrated on the composition of oratorios. He composed more than twenty in fewer than fourteen years. These included his most enduring work, *The Messiah*, written in 1741. Handel appeared as organ soloist at every one of his oratorio presentations, despite his blindness, which had become total by 1751. He died in 1759.

Handel was a very commercially minded individual who made money from teaching music as well as writing it.

Handel's contribution to opera

Handel produced fifty operas. After his death, they fell into neglect, but since the 1960s, with the revival of interest in baroque music, many of them have been recorded and performed onstage. He was responsible for great advances in musical coloration, combining brilliant vocal ornamentation with dramatically effective orchestral accompaniment. Arguably the finest of his operas is *Giulio Cesare* (1724) which, as a result of its superb orchestral and vocal writing, has entered the standard opera repertory.

Behavior at the theater

At this point, it is perhaps worth mentioning audience behavior, at both plays and operas, in 18th century England. There was no question of just sitting quietly and listening. During performances, audiences would chat, eat, play cards, heckle singers or actors they did not like, and cheer those that they did.

THEATRE   ROYAL

April   a Comedy   with the Muck Doctor
for the Benefit of the   Author of the Farce

Actors performing in a comedy at the Theatre Royal in the late 18th century, as depicted by William Hogarth. Audiences would routinely boo and heckle those players they did not like.

OPPOSITE: This 18th century engraving by William Hogarth of a performance of John Gay's *The Beggar's Opera* clearly demonstrates the chaotic, highly gregarious world that was the theater of the time.

Inside the theater

It seems normal to us to sit in semi-darkness at the theater or opera house, concentrating upon events on the stage. This is a relatively modern convention, however, that did not come into existence until the late 19th century. In the 18th century, the whole theater would be illuminated throughout a performance. People were there to be seen and attending the theater was a social occasion. The orchestra would often be in full display, rather than hidden in an orchestra pit. Those on stage would not be expected to remain in character throughout and once a particular aria was finished, it would not be uncommon for a singer to chat to friends in the audience.

Outbreaks of violence

Particular members of the nobility would have their own favorites and those who wished to ingratiate themselves would follow suit. Lord Burlington's followers, for example, supported Faustina Bordoni, while Lady Pembroke's faction favored Francesca Cuzzoni. Different cliques within the audience would noisily display their support and would even take violent action to support their favorites. It was not unusual for blows to be exchanged.

Temperamental stars

Star opera singers were also jealous of their status and did not take kindly to rivals. Faustina Bordoni and Francesca Cuzzoni famously resorted to pulling each other's hair on stage during a performance of Handel's *Astainate* in 1727.

Handel himself was not one to put up with the tantrums of singers. On one occasion, when Francesca Cuzzoni refused to sing a particular aria, he grabbed hold of her and pushed her forward until she hung out the window of the theater. *"Madam,"* he shouted, *"I know you are a true she-devil, but I will show you that I am Beelzebub, the chief devil."*

On another occasion, Handel had a heated exchange with the composer Johan Mattheson, which ended with swords being drawn.

want to know more?
The following CDs will give you a flavor of the music mentioned in this chapter:
- Lully: *Les Divertissements de Versailles* Erato: B000063TE8
- Rameau: *Les Indes galantes* Suites Musique d'abord: B00004TVGG
- Purcell: *Dido and Aeneas* Decca (US): B00004C8TE

4 From classical restraint to grand opera

The decades from the middle of the 18th to the middle of the 19th centuries were years of great political, economic, and artistic upheaval. It was the time of the Industrial Revolution, the American War of Independence, the French Revolution, and the Napoleonic Wars, the collapse of the ancien regime and the rise of the middle classes. This chapter deals with the developments in opera during these years, from the classicism of Gluck to the romanticism of Berlioz.

A lighter touch

Although the earliest operas had moments of humor and light relief, they were, in the main, serious in their subject matter. During the 18th century, however, a lighter style developed right across Europe—perhaps in response to the widening popularity of opera amongst the public at large.

Opera buffa

The new style of opera became known as *opera buffa*, as opposed to opera with more serious themes, which was called *opera seria*. Opera buffa tended to draw its stories from everyday life rather than classical mythology. The libretti were often based on texts by contemporary writers. Much of the dialog was spoken rather than sung or took the form of recitativo. In Germany, such opera was referred to as *Singspiel*, while in France the term *opéra comique* was used. John Gay's *The Beggar's Opera*, was an example of an English form known as ballad opera, in which spoken dialog was interspersed with songs set to popular melodies.

La Serva Padrona

The first great comic opera was *La Serva Padrona* (*The Landlady Servant*), composed in 1733 by Giovanni Battista Pergolesi. Originally performed as a two act intermezzo in his opera seria, *Il Prigionero Superbo*, it quickly became a popular work in its own right. When it was performed in Paris in 1752, it prompted the so-called *querelle des bouffons* (quarrel of the comedians) between supporters of serious French opera by Lully and Rameau and supporters of new

Italian comic opera. *La Serva Padrona* features characters that were to become staples of opera buffa, the *soubrette* and the *basso buffo*. The soubrette, a soprano, is a capricious young woman, usually a servant, who, despite her lighthearted nature, is always in control. In particular, she is always at least one step ahead of the lecherous older man, usually sung by a bass, who is pursuing her.

La Serva Padrona is a typical early example of opera buffa, featuring lechery, coquettish teasing, and a fairly predictable outcome.

The composers of opera buffa

The leading composers of opera buffa in the late 18th and early 19th centuries were the Italians Baldassare Galuppi (1706–1785), Niccolò Piccini (1728–1800), and Giovanni Paisiello (1740–1816). Piccini had great success in Paris, where his operas appealed to the taste for what was known as *comédie larmoyante* (tearful comedy). Paisiello traveled even more widely, working in Vienna, Paris, and St. Petersburg. It was in Russia that he wrote *Il Barbiere di Siviglia* (*The Barber of Seville*) in 1782, which, unfortunately for his reputation, was eclipsed by Rossini's later version in 1816.

must know

Comédie larmoyante was a genre of French drama in which imminent tragedy was averted in the end with tearful reconciliations. It was very popular in 18th century France, where audiences enjoyed seeing the heroes and heroines rewarded for the way in which they had endured their suffering throughout the piece.

The Gluckian reforms

Gluck was the first German composer to have a major influence on the development of opera. His aim was to make the drama of a work more important than the star singers who performed it. He argued for more restraint in stagecraft and a better balance between the different elements of opera.

Christoph Gluck was a torch-bearer for reform in 18th century opera, with an unusually broad experience of the medium.

Gluck

The son of a forester in the service of a nobleman, Christoph Willibald Gluck was born in Erasbach in Bavaria in 1714. As a young man, he studied music and philosophy in Prague, then, when he was 24, went to Milan to continue his education. It was here that he wrote his first opera, *Artaserse*, in 1741. He began to travel widely across Europe, visiting London, where he met Handel, in 1745. In 1754, he secured the post of Kapellmeister to Maria Theresa of Austria and settled in Vienna. In 1774, he spent five years in Paris, returning to Vienna where he died in 1787. Gluck's experience of opera in so many different countries led him to believe that it had become full of excesses that went against the original vision of the Camerata Fiorentina.

Gluck's reforms

Gluck set out his ideas on opera in the preface to the score of *Alceste* (1767). Here he wrote: *"I have striven to restrict music to its true office of serving poetry by means of expression and by following the situations of the story, without interrupting the action or stifling it with useless superfluity of ornaments."* Gluck emphasized the importance of the role of the orchestra, stressing that it should comment upon the action rather than merely accompanying the singers. He also made much more use of the chorus, using it to reflect upon events in the way that it would have done in Greek theater. In order to ensure continuity in his operas, he employed stage designers who could create sets that did not require constant changing.

Gluck's impact on the overture

Gluck's reforms also extended to the overture. This had previously served the function of entertaining the audience before the opera started, but did not necessarily relate to what was to follow. Gluck believed that the function of the overture was to create an atmosphere and to introduce the audience to the music that was to come. He therefore used material from the operas in his overtures, a practice that was to influence later composers such as Mozart, Beethoven, and Rossini.

Opera wars

Gluck's reforms met with violent opposition, particularly in Paris, where there was virtual war between supporters of Gluck and those who favored the opera buffa of Piccini. The directors of the Paris Opéra exploited this situation by deliberately persuading the two composers to treat the same subject, *Iphigénie en Tauride*, simultaneously. Gluck's *Iphigénie* was first produced in May 1779, with Piccini's version following in January 1781. Although performed seventeen times, the latter was afterwards consigned to oblivion, whilst Gluck's opera is generally recognized as his masterpiece. The bitter rivalry did not extend to the composers themselves, however, and on the death of Gluck, Piccini proposed that a public monument be erected in his honor.

must know

The term "classical" refers specifically to the art, literature, and architecture of ancient Greece and Rome. It is also used to describe the period in 18th century European culture when the perceived classical values of reason, balance, restraint, and strict adherence to form were admired and followed.

Mozart

While some of the composers discussed so far might be unfamiliar to those who are new to opera, there can be few who do not have at least a passing familiarity with the operas of Mozart. Like the plays of Shakespeare, they have become part of our common cultural heritage.

For many the greatest composer of all time—and certainly the creator of some of opera's most memorable works—Wolfgang Amadeus Mozart.

The genius of Mozart

Mozart ranks as one of the great geniuses of western civilization, his enormous output including every form of composition; symphonies, chamber music, sacred music, concertos, sonatas, and opera. He wrote operas in each style current in Europe: opera buffa, including *Le Nozze di Figaro* (The Marriage of Figaro) and *Così fan tutte*; dramma giocoso (*Don Giovanni*); opera seria, such as *Idomeneo* and *La clemenza di Tito* (*The Clemency of Titus*); and Singspiel, of which *Die Zauberflöte* (*The Magic Flute*) (pictured on page 40) is probably the most famous example by any composer. Just as Monteverdi gave artistic expression to the ideals of the Camerata, so Mozart realized the vision of Gluck, with his marriage of the elements of vocal and instrumental music, drama, characterization, and spectacle.

Mozart's early life

Born in Salzburg in 1756, Mozart was a child prodigy. His older sister, Maria Anna, was also talented, and the children's father, Leopold, exploited this dual ability. He took them "on the road," giving performances in the royal courts of Europe. The young Mozart was not only required to play; he also

performed musical "tricks," such as playing the clavier while a cloth was used to cover the keys. Leopold wanted to make sure that his son gained a good court position, but the unnatural life that he led retarded Mozart's normal growth to adulthood. As one of his earliest biographers said of him, *"He never learned to rule himself. For domestic order, for sensible management of money, for moderation and wise choice in pleasures, he had no feeling."*

The Vienna years

After an unhappy period of employment in the court of the Archbishop of Salzburg, Mozart settled in Vienna, determined to make his way in the world without relying upon unsympathetic employers. At first things went well. He took on pupils and his

***Don Giovanni* was immensely popular in its day and remains so today—a perfect example of Mozart's striving to combine drama with vocal excellence.**

OPPOSITE: **This image of a 2004 Canadian production of *The Marriage of Figaro* conveys all the satirical wit and human drama that Mozart and da Ponte sought to invest in their highly populist operatic tales.**

Singspiel, *Die Entführung aus dem Serail* (*The Abduction from the Seraglio*), was a great success in 1782. In the same year, he married Constanze Weber (having earlier been jilted by her sister Aloysia). In these early years in Vienna, Mozart enjoyed considerable success as a composer and performer. By 1785, when he was 29, he was among the best-paid musicians in Europe. From 1786 onward, however, he received fewer commissions and opportunities to perform. This was in part because he fell out of favor with those in power as a result of the pointed satire in *The Marriage of Figaro* of 1786 and partly because war with the Ottoman Empire had made economic conditions less favorable in Vienna. Unending poverty and illness plagued the family until Mozart's death, possibly from typhoid, in 1791. The place of his grave is unmarked.

An operatic partnership

Mozart's three great operas *Le Nozze di Figaro*, *Don Giovanni*, and *Così fan tutte* were written to librettos by Lorenzo da Ponte. While the librettist is often seen as a secondary partner, Mozart and da Ponte worked in a true collaborative relationship in producing their three joint operas. During the composition of *Don Giovanni*, for example, they occupied rooms on opposite sides of the same street in Prague and used to communicate with each other by calling back and forth. In their operatic collaborations, music and words are intrinsically linked. It must be remembered also that the subject matter of these operas—servants outwitting their masters, the search for sexual gratification, and the flouting of conventions—was revolutionary at the time.

Lorenzo da Ponte was born in Cenada, Italy, in 1749. After his collaboration with Mozart, he went to London and from there to New York, where he died in 1838.

The Magic Flute

Mozart's *Die Zauberflöte*, premiered in 1791, is the most famous example of the German form known as Singspiel. Although the story starts out as a romantic fairy tale, it later takes on a religious symbolism, reflecting the rites of the Masonic Order. (Mozart and his librettist, Emanuel Schikaneder, were both Masons.)

must know

Freemasonary is an organization sharing certain moral and metaphysical ideas and a belief in a supreme being. The first Grand Lodge formed in Freemasonry was The Grand Lodge of England, founded in 1717. Freemasonary was exported to the British Colonies in North America by the 1730s and appeared in France in 1728, spreading throughout the rest of Europe.

Act I

A handsome young Egyptian prince, Tamino, pursued by a vicious serpent, is saved by the three attendants of the Queen of the Night. The bird-catcher, Papageno, lies to Tamino, claiming that it was he who killed the serpent. The Queen of the Night herself gives Tamino the task of rescuing her daughter, Pamina, who has been abducted by the priest, Sarastro, in return for her hand in marriage. Papageno is to accompany him, their only aids being a magic flute and a set of protective bells. Arriving at the palace of Sarastro, Papageno foils Monostatos, a villainous servant, in his attempt to force himself on Pamina. Tamino, meanwhile, led by three spirits, finds Sarastro's temple and learns that he must join his cult in order to win Pamina. Relieved that she is still alive, he plays his flute and is answered in the distance by Papageno's pipes. As he rushes out to find his companion, Papageno and Pamina run in, but are intercepted by Monostatos. Only the music of Papageno's magic bells saves them from capture. Sarastro enters with his followers. Monostatos brings in the captured Tamino, but is sentenced to a whipping for his pains. Tamino and Pamina meet for the first time, but are separated until he and Papageno prove their worthiness.

Act II

Sarastro and his priests, discussing Tamino's and
Papageno's entry into their society, set the two men
dangerous tests to prove themselves. Pamina also
undergoes difficult trials, withstanding Monostatos'
unwelcome sexual advances. In this act, rather
inconsistently, the Queen of the Night is revealed as
evil and Sarastro as benevolent. Papageno fails the
tests, mostly because he is unable to keep quiet, but
his good nature wins him the beautiful bird-girl,
Papagena, as a wife. Pamina insists on accompanying
Tamino in his final ordeals, those of fire and water,
which they successfully complete. The Queen and
Monostatos fail in their final attempt to destroy the
Temple of Sarastro and the opera ends with a
celebration of love and the triumph of good over evil.

This contemporary production
of *The Magic Flute* captures all
the drama and pathos of one
of the best known of all operas.

The Romantic era

During the Romantic era, distinct styles of opera developed in France, Italy, and Germany, reflecting the ideals and beliefs of the Romantic movement. Grand Opera, an extravagant fusion of spectacle, action, music, and ballet, was the French expression of this Romanticism.

must know

Romanticism is the name given to a movement, developed toward the end of the 18th century, in which feeling was considered more important than reason. The Romantics idealized nature and folk traditions. Fascinated by the supernatural and the exotic, they championed the medieval over the classical world.

Grand Opera

From the time of Lully, Parisians had loved spectacle and elaborate stage machinery in opera. Grand Opera developed during the 19th century, following the fall of Napoleon, and reflected the tastes and values of the large Parisian middle-class. Everything in Grand Opera was on an epic scale—great heroism, great suffering, great passions, and huge crowd scenes. In keeping with Romantic ideals, the stories generally came from medieval and modern history rather than classical mythology.

Early examples of grand opera

Early examples of what was to become known as Grand Opera were *Lodoiska*, written in 1791 by Luigi Cherubini, *La Vestale* (1807), by Gasparo Spontini, and Daniel Auber's *La Muette da Portici* (*The Mute Girl of Portici*). The latter, first performed in 1828, is based on the story of an insurrection in Naples and concludes with an onstage eruption of Vesuvius. In 1830, a performance of this opera in Brussels actually sparked off a real insurrection that eventually led to the creation of the state of Belgium. The

The French composer Daniel Auber popularized the Romantic form of opera that was pioneered by the Italians Luigi Cherubini and Gasparo Spontini.

librettist for Auber's opera was the aptly named French writer Eugène Scribe, who was also responsible for producing the guidelines on which Grand Opera was based.

Luigi Cherubini

Luigi Cherubini had possibly the greatest influence on the early development of the musical form that was to become known as Grand Opera. Born in Florence in 1760, Cherubini began his musical education with his father, himself a musician, at the age of six. By the time he was thirteen, he had composed several religious works. In 1788, Cherubini settled in Paris, where he met with some success as a composer of opera. In 1805, he received an invitation from Vienna to write an opera and to direct it in person. *Faniska*, produced the following year, was enthusiastically received, in particular by Haydn and Beethoven, who considered him to be the greatest dramatic composer of the age. Cherubini died in Paris in 1842 at the age of 81.

must know

The mainly Catholic Belgians were at that time under Protestant Dutch rule and the plot of Auber's opera, concerning an uprising against the Spanish rulers of Naples in the 17th century, struck a chord with nationalists in the audience. As the crowd poured into the streets after a performance of the opera on August 25th, 1830, rioting broke out and the city hall was occupied. Dutch attempts to retake control by force failed and, following further street fighting over the next few weeks, the Belgians declared their independence in October.

Berlioz

Although he is generally now recognized as the greatest French composer of the 19th century, Berlioz did not meet with great success in his own country. He did, however, have influential admirers, including Wagner. He wrote only three operas, but the third of these, *Les Troyens*, is generally regarded as the greatest of all grand operas.

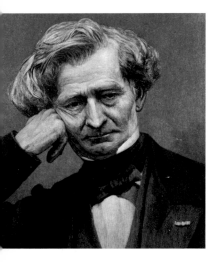

Hector Berlioz was not the most popular opera composer during his lifetime, but some of his works are regularly staged to this day.

The great Romantic

Hector Berlioz was a native of La Côte-Saint-André, between Lyon and Grenoble. His father was a doctor and the young Berlioz was sent to Paris to study medicine at the age of eighteen in 1821. He was horrified by the process of dissection, and, as he wrote, "leaped out of the window and fled home." Despite his father's disapproval, he abandoned medicine to study opera and composition at the Paris Conservatoire. He quickly became identified with the French Romantic movement and his friends included the writers Alexandre Dumas, Victor Hugo, and Honoré de Balzac. He was involved in a series of love affairs and, at the age of 23, his unrequited love for the actress Henrietta Constance Smithson was the inspiration for his *Symphonie Fantastique*. During his lifetime, Berlioz was better known as a conductor than as a composer. The unconventional nature of his music was not to the taste of Parisian audiences and Berlioz had to arrange for his own performances as well as pay for them himself. He died in 1869 and is buried in Montmartre, along with his two wives, Harriet Smithson and Marie Recio.

Les Troyens

Les Troyens (*The Trojans*) is a setting of the Dido and Aeneas story, for which Berlioz wrote his own libretto. It actually consists of two operas, *La Prise de Troie* (*The Capture of Troy*) and *Les Troyens à Carthage* (*The Trojans at Carthage*). The second of these had a number of performances in Paris in 1863 but the first was not staged until 1890, in Germany. In its monumental entirety, the opera lasts for six hours. In his memoirs, Berlioz accurately predicted the difficulties of staging this opera:

"I have just completed the poem and the music of Les Troyens, *an opera in five acts. The subject seems to me elevated, magnificent, and deeply moving— sure proof that the Parisians will find it dull and boring. Even supposing I am wrong to attribute to our public a taste so different from my own, I will not be able to find an intelligent and dedicated woman capable of interpreting the main role. It requires beauty, a great voice, genuine dramatic talent—a complete musician, with a soul and a heart of fire."*

The Death of Dido from *Les Troyens*. This was the most famous and acclaimed of Berlioz's operatic works.

Meyerbeer and Gounod

Although they are rarely performed nowadays, the operas of Giacomo Meyerbeer were enormously popular during his lifetime. Their fusion of melodramatic plots, dramatic music, and spectacular staging was a great hit with the Parisian public. Charles Gounod's *Faust* was similarly successful and remains so today.

Giacomo Meyerbeer was derided in some quarters because of his Jewish faith, but this did not diminish the popularity of his operas with the 19th century Parisian public.

From fame to neglect

Meyerbeer was born Jacob Liebmann Beer, in 1791, to a Jewish family in Tasdorf, near Berlin. The "Meyer" in his surname he adopted after the death of his great-grandfather, while he changed his first name to Giacomo after studying in Italy. He first became known internationally with his opera seria, *Il Crociato in Egitto*, but it was with *Robert le Diable* (*Robert the Devil*), produced in Paris in 1831, that he became a real star. This was followed by further successes with *Les Huguenots* (1836), *Le Prophète*

The conversion of Robert, Duke of Normandy, in the opera *Robert le Diable* by Giacomo Meyerbeer, painted in 1840 by Guillaume-Alphonse Harang (1814–84).

(1849), and *L'Africaine* (1865). Meyerbeer's operas were elaborate and very expensive to stage, featuring dramatic sets and ornate costumes, and they required large casts of singers. They were also subject to consistent attack from supporters of Wagner, who spread malicious rumors that his success was due to his bribing of musical critics. Wagner himself accused Meyerbeer of being interested only in money, not music. As a result, Meyerbeer's operas fell into neglect. His music was banned outright by the Nazis because he was a Jew. The operas are, however, now beginning to be revived and recorded.

As well as producing highly popular music, Meyerbeer kept extensive diaries and correspondence throughout his career which today make an important contribution toward our understanding of the music and theater of the time.

Gounod

Charles Gounod (1818–1893) was educated at the Paris Conservatoire, where he won the Prix de Rome in 1837. Since its first performance in Paris in 1859, his *Faust* has been one of the most popular of French operas and a worldwide favorite. It was the opera chosen to open the Metropolitan Opera in New York in 1883. Gounod's music captures all the excitement and menace of Goethe's story of magic and sex, as Faust is persuaded by Méphistophélès to barter his soul in exchange for all the pleasures of the world, including the love of the beautiful Marguerite. For a full account of the story behind Gounod's *Faust*, see the following pages 58–9.

want to know more?

- A budget price CD of Gluck's *Orfeo et Euridice* is available on Naxos B0000666A5
- Highlights of Mozart's operas can be found on *Mozart: Opera Highlights* Delta (US): B00001VRW Laserlight (UK) B00001VRW
- A three disc DVD of Berlioz's *Les Troyens* is available on BBC/Opus Arte: B0002TTTHO (all regions)

Charles Gounod took the perennially popular tale of Faust and turned it into an equally successful opera. However, few of his other works are remembered.

Faust

There is something in the Faust legend that has always appealed to writers and musicians. Among those who have offered interpretations of the story are Marlowe, Goethe, Mann, Wilde, Bulgakov, Berlioz, Wagner, Liszt, and, of course, Gounod, whose opera, *Faust*, premiered in Paris in 1859.

Faust is tempted by Méphistophélès in this poster promoting a 1925 production of Gounod's classic opera.

Act I

Méphistophélès appears to a suicidal Faust and, with a tempting image of a beautiful young girl, Marguerite, persuades him to accept his help in exchange for Faust's services in Hell. In the next scene, a chorus of soldiers and villagers sing a drinking song and Valentin, leaving for war, asks his friends Wagner and Siébel to protect his sister, Marguerite. Méphistophélès proposes a toast to Marguerite, which angers Valentin. He tries to strike Méphistophélès with his sword, but it shatters. The crowd raise the hilts of their swords as crosses to protect themselves. Méphistophélès is joined by Faust and the villagers in a waltz but Marguerite demurely refuses to take Faust's arm.

Act II

Siébel leaves a bouquet for Marguerite in her garden. Faust sends Méphistophélès in search of a better gift and he brings a box of jewels. Marguerite enters, thinking of her meeting with Faust and, seeing the jewels, tries them on. Méphistophélès flirts with a nosy neighbor so that Faust can get closer to Marguerite. She allows Faust to kiss her, but then asks him to leave. He does, but returns as she leans

from her window, singing of her love for him. Faust
goes to her and she submits, much to the
amusement of Méphistophélès.

Act III

Pregnant and abandoned, Marguerite tries to pray but
is stopped by the mockery of Méphistophélès. As the
chorus sings the *Dies Irae*, she begs for pardon, but in
vain. Valentin returns and, learning what has happened
to his sister, challenges Faust to a duel. He is killed, and
with his dying breath he condemns Marguerite to Hell.

Act IV

Méphistophélès and Faust are at a Walpurgis Night
feast when Faust sees a vision of Marguerite and asks
to be taken to her. He enters the prison where she is
being held for killing her child. As Faust urges her to
hurry away with him Marguerite recognizes
Méphistophélès as the Devil, hallucinates that Faust's
hands are covered in blood, rejects him, and faints.
Méphistophélès cries out that Faust has been judged.
Faust prays, while Marguerite's soul rises to heaven.

**A recent production of *Faust*,
featuring a moving projected
background and high-tech lighting.**

5 German opera in the 19th century

Before the late 18th century, German-language opera was largely a copy of Italian models. During the 19th century, however, it developed in a very different direction. Under the influence of Beethoven, German composers produced works in which the expression of private passions and personal ideals was all-important. German Romantic opera developed from the works of Weber to the "music dramas" of Wagner, arguably the most influential opera composer of all time.

Beethoven

Although he was only to write one opera, Beethoven's influence on other composers was enormous. In particular, his use of a larger orchestra gave him much greater powers of expression. Until then, the human voice had been the leading instrument, but in German opera, the orchestra now became an equal partner.

must know

Germany in the 19th century was a collection of separate states mainly under Austrian domination. In 1862, Wilhelm I of Prussia, the strongest of these states, appointed Count Otto von Bismarck as his chief minister. Bismarck achieved German unification under Prussia in less than ten years, after deliberately provoking wars with Denmark, Austria, and France. After the defeat of France, King Wilhelm was declared Kaiser (emperor) of Germany in the Hall of Mirrors at Versailles.

Beethoven's life and times

Ludwig van Beethoven was born in Bonn in 1770, moving to Vienna in his early twenties, where he studied with Joseph Haydn and quickly gained a reputation as a virtuoso pianist. He was inspired by the ideals of contemporary writers and thinkers, such as Goethe, Schiller, and Kant. Members of an artistic movement called *Sturm und Drang* (Storm and Stress), they loathed tyranny and advocated revolt against existing standards.

Beethoven believed that a musician did not exist to serve royal employers, but rather that his gifts should be shared with a wider public. He was determined that his music should not be a background to aristocratic gatherings but that it should be heard. He worked as a freelance composer, arranging subscription concerts, with the support of wealthy patrons who recognized his extraordinary talent.

In his late twenties Beethoven began to lose his hearing. Nevertheless, he continued to produce notable masterpieces throughout his life in the face of this personal disaster, even after his deafness became absolute. His anger and frustration at his condition resounds in much of his music.

Ludwig van Beethoven is better known for musical forms other than opera, but nevertheless he was hugely influential in the genre.

Fidelio

Beethoven's only opera involved considerable struggle on the composer's part, going through several revisions before achieving its final success. Like much of Beethoven's music of this time it emphasizes heroism. It also reveals Beethoven's strong sympathy of the contemporary struggle for political freedom. Highlights in the opera include the "Prisoners' Chorus," a song to freedom sung by a chorus of political prisoners, Florestan's hallucinatory vision of Leonore as an angel come to rescue him, and the finale, in which the soloists and chorus celebrate Leonore's valor.

must know

Johann Christoph Friedrich von Schiller (1759–1805) was a German poet, philosopher, and dramatist. His poem *An die Freude* (*Ode to Joy*) provides the text for the final movement of Beethoven's Ninth Symphony.

Immanuel Kant (1724–1804) was a German philosopher. He believed that we should think independently, free from the restraints of any external authority.

Fidelio's performance history

The first performance of Beethoven's only opera, then called *Leonore*, took place in Vienna on November 20th, 1805. It was somewhat affected by the fact that most of the audience consisted of officers of the French army that was occupying Vienna at the time. In the spring of 1806, a shortened version—in two acts rather than the original three—was staged, and although this was more successful, Beethoven became involved in a dispute with the theater management which prevented further

The famous scene in *Fidelio* in which the prisoners are released from captivity.

Leonore and Florestan are reunited in another scene of _Fidelio_.

performances. In 1814, Beethoven revised the opera yet again, this time adopting the name _Fidelio_. This version of the opera was, finally, a great success for Beethoven, and _Fidelio_ has been an important part of the operatic repertory ever since.

Fidelio's four overtures

As a result of the revisions that Beethoven made over a period of years, his opera has four different overtures. The first, for the 1805 performance, is now known as _Leonore No.2_. In 1806, he wrote a second version, _Leonore No.3_, which has entered the orchestral repertoire as a work in its own right. The overture referred to as _Leonore No.1_ was a revision for a planned performance in Prague in 1807. Finally, for the 1814 revival, Beethoven started again with fresh musical material and wrote what we now know as the _Fidelio_ overture.

Fidelio

Premiered in Vienna, just over a decade after *The Magic Flute*, Beethoven's *Fidelio* is the product of a very different social and historical context. The ideals of the French Revolution, carried throughout Europe by Napoleon's armies, are reflected in its attack on tyranny and its celebration of human nobility.

Act I

Jaquino, assistant to Rocco, the jailer of Seville's prison, is attempting to propose to the jailer's daughter, Marzelline. When he leaves, she expresses her love for Fidelio, Rocco's assistant, not knowing that Fidelio is actually Leonore, the wife of Florestan, a political prisoner. Believing that her husband is held captive in Seville she has disguised herself in order to find him. Pizarro, the governor of the prison,

Beethoven penned only one opera, but it is widely performed to this day. This US production was staged in 1987.

learns that Don Fernando, a government minister and friend of Florestan, is to pay a visit, suspecting that Pizarro is abusing his powers. He arranges for the murder of the secret prisoner. Leonore meanwhile persuades Rocco to allow the prisoners a chance to breathe the open air. They file onstage slowly, singing "The Prisoners' Chorus," a moving hymn to freedom. Pizarro, hearing of this unauthorized action, enters furiously and the prisoners are herded back into their cells.

Act II

In his cell, Florestan sings of his despair and sees a vision of Leonore leading him to Heaven. He faints as Rocco and Leonore descend into the cell and start digging a grave. Leonore realizes the prisoner is her husband, though he does not recognize her. Rocco gives a whistle to summon Pizarro, who, in the style of a true villain, pauses to gloat over his victim. As he draws his dagger, however, Leonore throws herself into his path, revealing herself as Florestan's wife and drawing a pistol. A trumpet call is heard offstage and Jaquino rushes in to announce the arrival of the minister, Don Fernando. Pizarro and Rocco quickly leave, while the reunited husband and wife sing a joyful duet. The short final scene takes place outside the prison, where Don Fernando frees all the prisoners. At this moment, Rocco brings in Florestan and Leonore. Don Fernando recognizes his old friend, whom he had thought dead. Pizarro is led away in chains and Don Fernando gives Leonore the privilege of removing the shackles from her husband. The opera closes with a chorus in praise of Leonore and the power of love.

German Romantic opera

Carl Maria von Weber provides the link between Beethoven and Wagner. He helped to create a new, distinctly German, tradition, influenced by the growth of Romanticism. His operas are stories of good and evil taken from German folklore, with characters whose fates are affected both by nature and the supernatural.

must know

In the literature, art, and music of German-speaking countries, German Romanticism was the dominant cultural movement of much of the 19th century. The Romantic movement developed later in Germany than in England, but found its greatest expression within that culture, exemplified by the work of the writers Heine, Schlegel, and others. In contrast to the seriousness of English romanticism, the German variety was lighter in tone, admitting fragmentation and incompleteness in its aesthetic theory as opposed to a quest for perfection and unity in all things.

Weber

Carl Maria von Weber was born in Eutin in 1786. The "von" was an affectation, as his family was not aristocratic. His mother was a singer and his father the director of a traveling theater company. Weber began his adult career as a concert pianist. The offer of a job conducting an opera house orchestra in Breslau gave him the opportunity to develop his understanding of orchestration. Subsequent posts included director of the Prague Opera and director of the Dresden Court Opera. Here he introduced various reforms and was a pioneer of the craft of conducting without the use of violin or keyboard instruments. Despite failing health, Weber continued directing, composing, and touring as a performer until his death from tuberculosis on June 5th, 1826, in London, where his final opera had premiered. His body was eventually returned to Dresden eighteen years later on the initiative of Richard Wagner, who made a graveside speech.

Weber's operas

Der Freischütz (*The Free Shooter*), which Weber wrote between 1817 and 1820, was the first great German Romantic opera. It is set in the wilds of the

forest, rather than the more elegant urban surroundings of Classical opera, and it has a strong supernatural element, especially in the famous "Wolf's Glen" scene. The music, which includes folk melodies, is powerful and evocative. The overture includes themes used later in the opera and associated with particular characters. In his second opera, *Euryanthe* (1823), Weber dispensed with spoken dialog and, reintroducing the arioso, set every word to music. Although he died shortly after writing his last opera, *Oberon*, in 1826, Weber was to have a profound influence on the development of German opera, and, in particular, on Richard Wagner.

A contemporary painting of action from the second act of Weber's *Der Freischütz*.

Wagner

Wagner is the most influential and controversial figure in the history of opera. Besides his operas, he wrote an enormous number of books and articles, ranging from theories of opera to political programs. Wagner's musical and dramatic innovations were revolutionary but, for many, these are overshadowed by his philosophical beliefs.

Richard Wagner as a young man, painted by Ernst August Becker, sometime in the 1840s.

OPPOSITE: Wagner's works are probably the best known in the entire canon of opera. Most music lovers have heard of the "Ride of the Valkyries" from his great Ring Cycle work *Die Walküre*.

Wagner's early life

As a youth, Wagner's ambition was to be a playwright and he first became interested in music as a means of enhancing his dramas. Born in Leipzig on May 22nd, 1813, he moved to Dresden the following year, after his father's death and his mother's remarriage. He enrolled at the University of Leipzig in 1831 to study music and his first opera, *Die Feen*, which imitated the style of Weber, was written in 1833 (though it was not performed until after his death). He held brief appointments as musical director in opera houses and in 1836 married Christine Planer. They moved to Riga, but amassed such debts that they were forced to leave in 1839. The following two years were spent in Paris, where Wagner completed *Der Fliegende Holländer* (*The Flying Dutchman*) and *Rienzi*. There followed a move to Dresden (and the composition of *Lohengrin*) which ended in flight yet again, following Wagner's involvement in radical politics.

Exile and inspiration

Wagner spent the next twelve years in exile. Isolated and in a miserable financial state, he began work on the sketches that would eventually become his monumental Ring Cycle, *Der Ring des Nibelungen*,

Like *Die Walküre* (which is also pictured on page 60), *Das Rheingold* is part of Wagner's greatest work, the vast and unparalleled *Der Ring des Nibelungen* (The Ring Cycle).

and a series of essays outlining his artistic philosophy. In 1857, an infatuation with the poet Mathilde Wesendonk was the inspiration for *Tristan und Isolde*, the dissonant opening notes of which many musicologists claim to be the beginning of "modern" music. In 1861, with the political ban against him lifted, Wagner settled in Biebrich, Prussia, where he began work on *Die Meistersinger von Nürnberg* (*The Mastersingers of Nuremburg*) and separated from his wife. In 1864, he received a summons from King Ludwig II to come to Bavaria. The eccentric young ruler was passionately in love with Wagner's music and probably with Wagner himself. A year later, however, he was obliged to go into exile again, following a series of scandals, notably his affair with Cosima von Büllow, Lizst's daughter and the wife of the conductor of the Munich Court Opera, whom he finally married in 1870.

Wagner's later years

Good relations were eventually restored with Ludwig and plans were discussed for the building of a new opera house, where the completed Ring Cycle could finally be staged. The Bayreuth Festspielhaus (Festival House) was finally opened in August 1876. In 1877, Wagner began work on *Parsifal*, his last opera. During this period, he also wrote a series of increasingly reactionary essays on religion and art. *Parsifal* was completed in January 1882 and a second Bayreuth Festival was held for the new opera. Wagner was by this time extremely ill. During the final performance of *Parsifal*, he secretly entered the orchestra pit during Act III, took the baton from conductor Hermann Levi, and led the performance to its conclusion. Five months later, he died in Venice. His body was returned to Bayreuth for burial.

The epic themes of Wagner's work resonate throughout the Ring Cycle, and are no better exemplified than by Siegfried's slaying of Fafner the Dragon.

Tristan and Isolde

Wagner's opera finally had its premiere in 1865, six years after its completion. He called it a "music drama," for the usual operatic pattern of arias, duets, and choruses was replaced by what Wagner referred to as "endless melodizing," with the orchestra playing as important a part as the singers.

Act I

Aboard Tristan's ship, Isolde, a princess of Ireland, and her handmaid, Brangaene, are being taken to Cornwall, where Isolde is to be married to King Marke. Isolde's fiancé, Morold, had been killed by Tristan, whom she had unknowingly nursed back to health. Realizing who he was, she had resolved to kill him, but had fallen in love instead. She sends Brangaene to command Tristan to appear before her, but he refuses. Furious, she decides to kill both him and herself. When he does appear, she offers him a drink. Expecting it to be poisoned, he accepts. She drinks the other half, but Brangaene has substituted the poison with a love potion. They look longingly into each other's eyes, as the sailors announce that land has been sighted.

Act II

It is nightime, and Tristan and Isolde have planned to meet while King Marke is off hunting. Alone at last, they declare their passion for each other. Tristan claims that daylight keeps them apart and it is only at night that they can be together. He prophetically compares night to death and says that only in the long night of death can they be eternally united.

Finally, as day breaks, King Marke, led by Tristan's treacherous friend Melot, returns to find Tristan and Isolde in each others arms. Melot and Tristan fight, but Tristan throws down his sword and is fatally wounded.

Tristan and Isolde **comprises many of the essential elements of classic Wagnerian opera, although its composer referred to it as a "music drama."**

Act III

Tristan has been brought home to Brittany by his servant Kurwenal. A ship bringing Isolde to him is sighted and Tristan, in his excitement, tears the bandages from his wounds. Isolde is almost too late, for as she embraces him, he dies. A ship bearing Melot, Marke, and Brangaene arrives and Kurwenal furiously attacks Melot to avenge Tristan. In the fight, both are killed. Marke and Brangaene finally reach Isolde and Marke explains that he has been told about the love-potion by Brangaene. He had come to unite the lovers, not to part them. Isolde dies of grief, holding Tristan's body in her arms.

Gesamtkunstwerk

This German term, meaning "total art work," refers to the way in which Wagner's operas blend music, drama, staging, and philosophy into a seamless whole. It is best revealed in the Ring Cycle. This vast work consists of four operas—*Das Rheingold*, *Die Walküre*, *Siegfried*, and *Götterdämmerung* (*The Twilight of the Gods*).

The Ring

The story follows the struggles of gods, heroes, and a collection of mythical figures over the possession of a magic ring that grants domination over the entire world. The drama continues through three generations, until the final cataclysm at the end of *Götterdämmerung*. For the staging of this work, Wagner placed great importance on such elements as a darkened theater and seating arrangements that focused the attention of the audience on the stage— revolutionary ideas at the time. He adopted a through-composed style, where each act of each opera would be a complete unit with no breaks whatsoever.

This photograph of a 1990 production of *Das Rheingold* perfectly demonstrates Wagner's goal to focus attention on the stage through the use of contrasting lighting and striking sets.

Grundthemen

Wagner used what he called *Grundthemen* (now generally referred to as leitmotifs) as a unifying device. These are recurring melodies or harmonies that denote a character, object, emotion, or other subject mentioned in the text. While other composers before Wagner had already used leitmotifs, the Ring Cycle was unique in the extent to which he employed them. He also weakened traditional tonality so that most of the Ring cannot be said to be in "keys" as traditionally defined, but rather in "key areas," each of which flows smoothly into the following one. The Ring called for an orchestra far larger than any that had been previously used in opera. To achieve the effects he wanted, he introduced new instruments, such as the Wagner tuba, which fills the gap between the French horn and the trombone.

The large-scale, grandiose settings of *Götterdämmerung* are typical of Wagner's operatic *Gesamtkunstwerk*.

Wagner's anti-semitism

In the 20th century, particularly in Israel and the United States, Wagner's reputation was clouded by his anti-semitism. He believed that the Germans were members of a superior race who had been deprived of their rightful place by inferior peoples, especially the Jews.

Wagner's essays

Wagner frequently accused Jews of being an alien element in German culture. His essay *Das Judenthum in der Musik* (*Jewishness in Music*), was an attack on composers such as Mendelssohn and Meyerbeer in which he argued that their music was shallow because they had no connection to "the genuine spirit of the Volk." In calling for the eradication of Jewish culture he used the chilling phrase *"only one thing can redeem you from the burden of your curse: the redemption of going under!"*. Wagner did choose a Jew, Hermann Levi, to conduct *Parsifal*, though he also tried to persuade him to be baptized as a Christian.

The tenor Plácido Domingo in the title role of *Parsifal*, Wagner's final opera (below and opposite). This futuristic production was staged by the Los Angeles Opera.

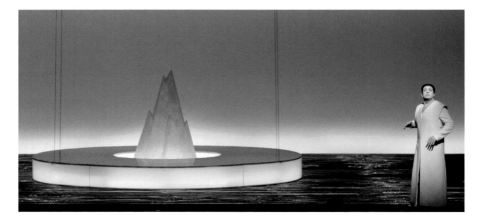

German music and the Nazis

Adolf Hitler said of Wagner, *"Whoever wants to understand National Socialistic Germany must know Wagner."* Hitler's obsession with Wagner has done the composer's reputation no good at all. To be fair, however, he was not the only German composer to be adopted by the Nazis. The party newspaper, the *Völkischer Beobachter*, also referred to Handel as *"the earliest and most effective champion of German music in foreign lands."* He had obviously not settled in England to make money, but to *"[carry] forth the musical impetus of nordic England, which had been asleep since Henry Purcell's death, into the great German stream of nordic creative power."* The same newspaper also carried an article entitled "The German Soldier Is Also Protecting Mozart's Music," while, on the orders of the Nazis, new libretti were written for the operas in which Mozart had collaborated with the Jewish da Ponte.

want to know more?

To learn more about the controversy over Wagner's anti-semitism, find the article by Lili Eylon on the following website:
www.jewishvirtual library.org

For a taste of the highlights of Wagner's music try this CD:
The Best of the Ring
Philips (US): B00000041EJ
Duo (UK): B00000041EJ

6 Italian opera in the 19th century

While opera in France tended toward spectacle, Italian opera continued to place the main emphasis on the voice. Italian composers believed that the voice is the most important element in opera, with the sound more important than the words. The musical style known as bel canto, or "beautiful singing," was developed by composers such as Bellini, Donizetti, and Rossini. Towering over Italian opera in this century, however, was the giant figure of Giuseppe Verdi.

Bel canto

Bel canto singing is characterized by its focus on perfect evenness throughout the vocal range, skilful legato, great ornamental agility, and a soft, rounded tone. Operas in the style feature much ornamentation, with fast scales and cadenzas, and a stress on technique rather than volume.

Domenico Donizetti pioneered change in Italian opera in the 19th century through the development of the bel canto form.

Features of bel canto opera

Bel canto arias often have two sections. The *cavatina* is slow and melodic, while the *cabaletta* is usually faster and gives the singer the opportunity for a display of vocal technique. It often ends with a crowd-pleasing, soaring high note. The chorus plays a more important role in bel canto opera, interacting with the soloist and commenting on, or seconding, what he or she has expressed. Another bel canto specialty was the "mad scene," in which the soprano portrays insanity or despair through a display of spectacular vocal effects. Famous examples of such scenes are to be found in Donizetti's *Lucia di Lammermoor* and Bellini's *I Puritani*, both first staged in 1835.

Donizetti and Bellini

Domenico Gaetano Maria Donizetti (1797–1848) was the child of a very poor family with no tradition of music. He is best known for his operatic works, but he also wrote church music, a number of string quartets, and some orchestral works.

The family of the Sicilian, Vincenzo Salvatore Carmelo Francesco Bellini (1801–1835), was very musical and he was a child prodigy. After studying in

Naples, he moved to Milan in 1827, where he had great success, until his untimely death in Paris in 1835. First buried in Père Lachaise, his body was later moved to his home town of Catania. Bellini is best known for his opera *Norma*, the title role of which is considered by many to be the most difficult in the soprano repertoire.

The role of Norma was created for the great Italian soprano Giuditta Pasta (1797–1865). During the 20th century only a handful of singers, including Joan Sutherland and Maria Callas, were able to overcome its technical demands successfully.

Donizetti's *Lucia di Lammermoor* was a classic example of how the bel canto singing method could be used to heighten a sense of great drama and suspense.

Rossini

The fact that his best known works are comedies, combined with the alleged ease with which he wrote them, has sometimes led to Rossini being viewed as a lightweight composer. He occupied an unrivaled position in the Italian musical world of his time, however, and can rightly be regarded as one of the greatest composers of his era.

Rossini was unusually prolific for a composer of opera, but the quality of his output is undeniable.

The life and times of Rossini

Gioacchino Rossini's father was a horn player, while his mother made a career for herself in opera. He was born in Pesaro in 1792 and, as a boy, was exposed to operatic performance, both in the orchestra pit and on stage. Until 1823, his operas were first performed in Italy. There followed a period of success in France, leading to his final opera, *Guillaume Tell*, being staged in Paris in 1829. Although he wrote no further operas, he continued to enjoy considerable esteem, both in Paris and in Italy, where he spent the years from 1837 until 1855. He finally returned to France, where he died in 1868.

Rossini's operatic works

Rossini wrote some forty operas between 1810 and 1829. *L'Italiana in Algeri* (*The Italian in Algiers*), *Il Barbiere di Siviglia* (*The Barber of Seville*), and *La Gazza Ladra* (*The Thieving Magpie*) show his skill at writing opera buffa, but he could also create opera seria, as illustrated by *Tancredi and Mosè in Egitto* (*Moses in Egypt*). During his own lifetime, the most popular of all his operas was *Guillaume Tell* (*William Tell*). By 1868, it had already been performed no fewer than five hundred times in Paris. Although rarely performed uncut nowadays, its large scale romantic drama anticipates the works of Verdi and Wagner. Rossini's operas are characterized by sparkling melodies, brilliant comic timing, and the expressive role of the orchestra. A particular innovation of his was the dramatic use of crescendi. This popular feature of his music earned him the nickname "Monsieur Crescendo."

Rossini's overtures

Apart from the comedies, most of Rossini's works fell into neglect after his death. Even those who know little about opera, however, are aware of his overtures, many of which have outlasted the operas for which they were composed. Rossini's reputed laziness and the speed with which he could compose when necessary are illustrated by a series of stories he told himself about his overtures (see box, above right).

must know

Rossini was apparently very laid-back about his work, as this and other observations reveal: *"I wrote the overture of Otello in a small room of the Palazzo Barbaja, where the baldest and rudest of directors had shut me in."*

A set design for Act III of the opera *Guillaume Tell* by Rossini, performed on August 3rd, 1829 at the Paris Opéra Garnier.

The Barber of Seville

The first performance of Rossini's *Il Barbiere di Siviglia*, in Rome on February 20th, 1816, was a disaster. Thirty years earlier, Giovanni Paisiello had produced a popular version of the same story which distinctly overshadowed the premiere of Rossini's version. Nevertheless, Rossini's *Barbiere* became a great success and remains one of the most popular of all operas.

Act I

Figaro is persuaded to help his former employer, Count Almaviva, who has adopted the guise of Lindoro, a poor student, in order to woo the beautiful Rosina. She is under the constant watch of her guardian, Doctor Bartolo, who has decided to marry her himself. Figaro suggests that Almaviva disguise himself as a drunken soldier with a faked document ordering that he be billeted at Bartolo's house. Figaro, as Bartolo's barber, has free access to the house and takes advantage of this to speak to Rosina about Lindoro. However, Don Basilio, a music teacher, has told Bartolo the identity of Rosina's secret lover and the two plot to discredit him. The scene becomes more complicated when Almaviva enters. Bartolo attempts to remove him and he slips Rosina a note in the confusion. Eventually, the police are called, but Almaviva reveals his identity to their officer and is released.

Act II

The Count disguises himself as Don Alonso, a music tutor, convincing Bartolo that he was sent as a substitute by the sick Don Basilo. During the music

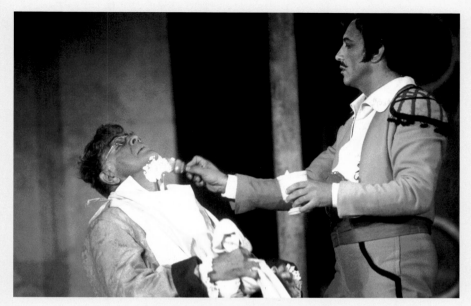

lesson, Figaro arrives to shave the Doctor and further distract his attention from the blossoming romance. Don Basilio enters at this moment, clearly not indisposed, though the other characters convince him that he is suffering from scarlet fever. Bartolo's suspicions are aroused, however, and he hurries everyone out of the room. Determined to marry Rosina at once, he sends Basilio to get the notary, while he goes for the watchmen, planning to have the conspirators arrested when they come for Rosina. The count and Figaro enter, muffled in cloaks, prepared for the elopement, but find that Bartolo has removed the ladder they had prepared. When Basilio arrives with the notary, the count bribes them to officiate at a different wedding instead. Bartolo returns with the watchmen to find Almaviva and Rosina already married. The outwitted doctor is mollified when he is told that he will be allowed to keep Rosina's dowry and the opera ends amidst general rejoicing.

Figaro shaves the Doctor in one of the most famous scenes in all opera.

Verdi

Giuseppe Verdi was one of the giants of 19th century opera and his works still form a major part of the standard repertoire. He lived through a period of great political upheaval in Italy and the enormous impact of his operas had much to do with this.

A peerless composer of popular masterpieces, Giuseppe Verdi is an Italian national hero to this day.

Political background

When Verdi began writing his operas, Italy as an independent nation did not exist. In 1850, it was still a collection of separate states ruled by foreign powers, principally Austria. One state, however, Piedmont-Sardinia, was independent. Its king, Victor Emmanuel, was dedicated to achieving Italian unification. Partisans, who wanted Victor Emmanuel to conquer Milan, gave their campaign a codename: "Viva VERDI." Verdi was a secret acronym for Vittorio Emanuele Re D'Italia, referring to Victor Emmanuel, King of Italy. This enabled nationalists to freely shout their support for Victor Emmanuel, while outsiders assumed they were fans of the composer. Verdi was aware of this use of his name and is believed to have consented. The wild success of *Nabucco* in particular put Verdi's name and music in the minds of many Italians at the time. The opera's "Chorus of the Hebrew Slaves," the lament of captives in Babylonia, was an immense success. Also known as *Va' Pensiero*, from its first line, the song has become a second Italian national anthem. When Italy was finally unified, Verdi became a deputy in the country's first parliament.

Verdi's early years

The son of an innkeeper, Verdi was born in 1813 in Le Roncole, a village near Busseto in the province of Parma. He went to Milan when he was twenty to continue his studies, but the Conservatory of Music rejected him. Instead, he took private lessons in counterpoint and also started attending opera performances. Returning to Busseto, he became town music master and he gave his first public performance in 1830 at the home of a local merchant and music lover, Antonio Barezzi, who invited him to be the music teacher of his daughter, Margherita. She and Verdi married in 1836. The production of his first opera, *Oberto*, in Milan achieved a degree of success, after which Bartolomeo Merelli, an impresario with La Scala, offered Verdi a contract for two more works. While working on his second opera, *Un Giorno di Regno*, Verdi's wife and children died. The opera was a flop and he fell into despair, vowing to give up musical composition forever. Merelli persuaded him to write *Nabucco* in 1842, however, and its opening performance made Verdi famous.

The "galley years"

After the deaths of his wife and children, Verdi threw himself into his work. He described this period as his *anni di galera* (galley years). During the years from 1843 to 1850, he wrote thirteen operas, including *Macbeth*, the first of his adaptations of Shakespeare, in 1847. He gave Lady Macbeth a more significant role than Shakespeare did, and the moment of her sleepwalking is one of opera's great "mad scenes." Verdi was, by this time, unchallenged as Italy's leading composer, but his greatest works were still to come.

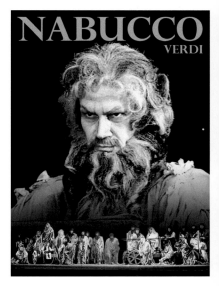

A poster promoting a 2005 production of Verdi's *Nabucco* by the Chisinau National Opera, staged in Belfast, Northern Ireland.

The late operas

Between 1851 and 1853, Verdi produced the three masterpieces *Rigoletto* (1851, pictured on page 80), *Il Trovatore* (1853), and *La Traviata* (1853). He had problems with the Italian censors over the subject matter of both *Rigoletto* and *La Traviata*, the former because of its political overtones (the censors felt that it encouraged anti-monarchist feelings), the latter for its portrayal of sex and prostitution. At the time, Verdi was living with the singer Giuseppina Strepponi, who had been in the cast of *Nabucco* and whom he finally married in 1859. *Les Vêpres Siciliennes* (*The Sicilian Vespers*) (1855) and *Simon Boccanegra* (1857) were somewhat overshadowed

must know

La Traviata was based upon the novel *La Dame aux Camélias* by Alexandre Dumas, *fils*, which was published in 1848. Its first performance was staged in Venice on March 6th, 1853. The title means literally "The Woman Who Strayed." It is an immensely popular work, which according to Opera America is the third most performed opera in the USA, behind only *Madame Butterfly* and *La Bohème*.

The political overtones of Verdi's later works reflected the troubled times in which he lived—none more so than those of *Rigoletto*.

by the operas that came before and after. He wrote *Un Ballo in Maschera* (*A Masked Ball*) in 1859, *La Forza del Destino* (*The Force of Destiny*) in 1862, *Don Carlos* in 1867, and *Aïda*, to celebrate the opening of the Suez Canal, in 1871. He then retired, but was persuaded back to produce his final Shakespearean operas, *Otello* (1887) and *Falstaff* (1893). He spent the remaining years of his life in Milan, where he died in 1901, a beloved national figure.

Verdi's masterpiece *Aïda* is one of the most spectacular of all operas, featuring a huge cast and lavish, monumental sets.

The legacy of Verdi

Verdi took Italian opera to new heights of dramatic expression. His works remain popular for their emotional intensity, dramatic vigor, tuneful melodies, and characterization. He took the traditions of Italian opera and transformed them into a unified musical and dramatic entity. Although often attacked by the critics—both in his own lifetime and today—for catering to the tastes of the masses, Verdi's masterpieces still dominate the standard repertoire.

want to know more?

To learn more about the Italian struggle for unification, try *Italian Unification 1820-71* by Martin Collier, (Heinemann, 2003)

For a taste of the highlights of Verdi's operas try *The Best of Verdi Operas* Prism Leisure (US): BoooAo6VYY Platinum (UK): BoooAo6VYY

Aïda

The opera was commissioned by Ismail Pasha, Khedive of Egypt, and was first performed in Cairo on December 24th, 1871. Production was delayed by the Franco-Prussian war and Verdi donated a portion of his considerable fee to the victims of the siege of Paris.

Act I

Aïda, daughter of the Ethiopian King Amonasro, is enslaved in Egypt. Since her capture, she has fallen in love with Radames, a young warrior, who has similar feelings for her. Unfortunately, the King's daughter, Amneris, is also in love with him. When news comes that the Ethiopians are invading Egypt, led by Amonasro, Radames is chosen to lead the Egyptians into battle, urged on by Amneris. Aïda, however, is torn between love for Radames and for her father.

Act II

The Ethiopians have been defeated and Amneris uses this as an opportunity to find out whether Aïda is her rival, as she suspects. Feigning sympathy with Aïda for the defeat of her people, she pretends that Radames has been killed. Aïda's reaction tells her all she wants to know. There follows the famous Triumphal Scene as Radames returns victorious, leading the Ethiopian captives, Amonasro among them. The Egyptian king grants Radames anything he wishes and, out of his love for Aïda, he asks for the captives to be released. Aïda and Amonasro, however, remain as hostages to ensure that the Ethiopians do not seek revenge. The king then rewards Radames by betrothing him to his daughter.

Act III

Aïda comes to the banks of the Nile for a last meeting with her lover on the evening before his wedding. First, however, her father appears and persuades her to obtain strategic information from Radames. Radames appears and eventually agrees to run away with Aïda. He tells her the position of the guards they must avoid. This is what Amonasro wanted to know. Amneris and the priest emerge from the temple, Aïda and her father flee, and Radames allows himself to be taken prisoner.

Act IV

Amneris pleads with the priests to show mercy to Radames but their sentence is that he shall be buried alive. Aïda has hidden herself in the crypt to die with him. They accept their terrible fate, bid farewell to lfe's sorrows, and await their death. Above their tomb, Amneris weeps and prays while the priests continue their jubilant celebrations.

Act One, Scene One of possibly the most famous and best-loved of Verdi's operas.

7 The development of national styles

During the 19th century, as the old empires started to crumble, the modern nations of Europe were slowly emerging. Nationalism was a potent force in the second half of the century. This was reflected in music, as national operas were created in the local language and based on indigenous stories and legends. Recognizable national styles developed in Russia, eastern Europe, and France, while in Italy, a new, realistic style—*Verismo*—appeared.

Opera in Russia

Opera had reached Russia by the early 18th century. Most operas were in Italian, although a Russian version of *Orpheus and Euridice*, *Orfey i Evridika*, was written by Evstigney Fomin in 1792. Russian opera as a distinct national style, however, is generally agreed to have begun with Mikhail Ivanovich Glinka.

must know

Evstigney Ipatovich Fomin was born in St. Petersburg in 1751. After studying music in St. Petersburg, he went to Italy in 1782. Returning to Russia in 1785 he composed about thirty operas, including *Yamshchiki na podstave* (*The Coachmen at the Relay Station*) in 1787 and the comic opera *Amerikansi* (*Americans*) in 1800, the year in which he died. His final opera *Zolotoya Yabloko* (*The Golden Apple*) was staged posthumously in 1803.

Glinka's influences

Glinka was born in the village of Novospasskoye in June 1804 into a family with a long tradition of service to the Tsar. As a child, he was pampered by his grandmother and developed a sickly disposition which he retained into later life. From birth, he was surrounded by folk songs and the music of the Russian Orthodox Church. Following the death of his grandmother, he was moved to the estate of his uncle, where he was exposed for the first time to the music of Haydn, Mozart, and Beethoven. At the age of thirteen, he was sent to study in St. Petersburg, where he had piano lessons from the English composer John Field.

Glinka's operas

From 1830, Glinka traveled in Italy and Germany, returning to Russia in 1836, where he composed *Zhizn' za tsarya* (*A Life for the Tsar*). The opera, about a peasant who sacrifices his life to save the Tsar from Polish invaders, uses native folk song to represent Russian heroism and Polish mazurkas and

Mikhail Glinka was a pioneer of cultural change in Russia whose importance to the emergence of a distinctive Russian form of opera is comparable to that of Pushkin in Russian literature.

A program cover for a production of Glinka's *A Life for the Tsar*, dating from 1836.

polonaises to represent the invading forces. His second, and final, opera *Ruslan i Ludmila* (*Ruslan and Lyudmila*) was premiered in 1842. It was based on a story by Pushkin, Russia's greatest poet and widely regarded as the father of Russian literature. It was not a success at first, though the overture has become an orchestral showpiece, but its combination of western compositional style and Russian folk elements had a great influence on future Russian opera. In later life, Glinka traveled to France, where Berlioz conducted excerpts from his operas. From there he moved to Berlin, where he died in 1857.

The Five

The teacher of composition at the St. Petersburg Conservatory was a German called Zaremba, who dismissed Glinka and his followers as "savages and candle-eaters," regarding them as primitive and unsophisticated in their methods. Opposed to him was a group of composers known as "The Five," who were dedicated to composing music with a specifically Russian flavor.

must know

The original Russian name for "The Five" was *"Moguãaja kuãka"* (The Mighty Handful). Their loose collaboration began in 1856, with the first meeting of Mily Alexeyevich Balakirev and César Cui; Modest Mussorgsky joined them in 1857, Nikolai Rimsky-Korsakov in 1861, and Alexander Borodin in 1862.

Mussorgsky

Modest Petrovich Mussorgsky was the child of a wealthy family, reputedly descended from Rurik, the first Russian ruler. Born in 1839, his intended career was as a military officer, but he resigned his commission in 1858 and, the following year, assisted in a production of Glinka's *A Life for the Tsar*, after which he professed a love for "everything Russian." After several abandoned opera projects, he began work on *Boris Godunov*, a psychological study of the

Modest Mussorgsky's considerable talent was ravaged by alcoholism and he died at a young age.

Mussorgsky's turbulent masterpiece *Boris Godunov* is certainly the most famous of The Five's work outside Russia.

disturbed Tsar based on a story by Pushkin. It was finally produced in St. Petersburg in 1874 and, although it was not a complete critical success, it marked the peak of his career. In the years following, his health declined rapidly, in part due to his alcoholism, and he died in 1881, a week after his forty-second birthday. *Boris Godunov* was revised by Rimsky-Korsakov in 1896 and again in the 20th century by Shostakovitch, who also adapted it for film.

Borodin

Alexander Porfirevich Borodin was the illegitimate son of a Georgian prince, Luka Semyonovich Gedeanishvili, who had him registered as the son of one of his serfs, Porfiry Borodin. Born in St. Petersburg in 1833, he had a good musical education but gained a degree in medicine and pursued a career in chemistry. He later described himself as a "Sunday composer." In 1869, he turned from working on his second symphony to begin his

must know

It is interesting to note that the least well known of The Five— Mily Alexeyevich Balakirev (1837–1910)— was actually the man responsible for bringing the group together in the first place. His own music has faded into obscurity, with the possible exception of his *Islamey: An Oriental Fantasy*, which is still popular among pianists.

Alexander Borodin's principal career was as a chemist and he regarded himself as a part-time composer. His formal demeanor belied a checkered upbringing.

opera *Knâz' Igor* (Prince Igor), based on a 12th century Slavic epic poem. He worked on it for seventeen years and it was still incomplete at his death in 1887. Completed posthumously by Rimsky-Korsakov and Alexandr Glazunov, it is not widely known outside Russia, apart from the Polovetsian Dances, which are often performed as an independent orchestral work.

Rimsky-Korsakov

A native of Novgorod, where he was born in 1844, Nikolai Andreyevich Rimsky-Korsakov studied at the Imperial Naval College and became an officer in the Russian navy. A prolific composer, he wrote fifteen operas whose subjects range from historical drama to folk opera, fairytales, and legends. They have remained part of the standard repertoire in Russia, but in the West they are best known for orchestral selections, such as "Dance of the Tumblers" from *Snegurochk* (*The Snow Maiden*) and 'Flight of the Bumble Bee' from *Skazka o care Saltane* (*The Tale of Tsar Saltan*). His opera *Zolotoy Petuschok* (*The Golden Cockerel*) upset the censors with its apparent criticism of monarchy. He died in 1908 and was buried in St. Petersburg.

With the exception of Mussorgsky's *Boris Godunov*, it is Nikolai Rimsky-Korsakov's operatic works which are best known outside Russia.

César Cui

César Cui (1835–1918) was of French and Lithuanian descent and his works are not so obviously Russian as those of the other members of The Five, although he did draw on Pushkin for sources. His work is little known in the West, apart from his children's opera *Kot v sapogakh* (*Puss in Boots*) which has had some success in Germany.

Boris Godunov

Mussorgsky's opera exists in numerous versions. He made two himself, while Rimsky-Korsakov made two more. The opera was re-orchestrated by Shostakovich in 1959. The story remains roughly the same in all versions, with the Russian people, depicted in the great choral scenes, acting as a second principal character.

must know

In 1580 the real Boris Godunov's sister married Feodor, the son of Ivan the Terrible. On Ivan's death, Boris was appointed as Feodor's guardian. A rebellion in favour of Dmitri, the son of Ivan's fifth wife, was put down and Dmitri was exiled. His death in 1591 is generally attributed to Boris, who seized the throne in 1598 on the death of Feodor.

Prologue

The regent, Boris Godunov, is urged to take the throne, following the death of Ivan the Terrible's two sons, one of whom, Dmitri, was murdered by Boris. The people are ordered to pray that Boris becomes Tsar. He refuses at first, but then assumes the title, amidst great rejoicing.

Act I

Five years later, a young monk, Gregory, learns the rumor of the murdered Dmitri and conceives the idea of seeking power as a pretender. In Scene II, at an inn near the Lithuanian border, Gregory enters with two monks who have escaped from the monastery with him. Shortly afterward a policeman appears, searching for a runaway whose description matches that of Gregory. He rushes from the room with the policeman in pursuit.

Act II

Things are going badly in Russia and everyone blames the Tsar, who is racked with guilt over the murder of Dmitri. Word is brought to him that a man claiming to be Dmitri is rousing the people. Boris's guilt turns into hallucinations and madness.

Act III

In a garden before the Polish castle of Mniszech, the false Dmitri is urged to attack Moscow by Marina, the daughter of a Polish noble. She wishes to become Tsarina and the Jesuit priest, Rangoni, tells her she must enslave the pretender with her beauty and bring Russia under the dominion of Rome.

Boris Godunov rails against the world in this oft-repeated tale of power, madness, and murder.

Act IV

The Russian nobles are discussing the false Dmitri's revolt. Prince Shuiski tells how he saw Boris hallucinating about the dead Tsarevich. Boris enters, protesting his innocence, but upon hearing the story of a blind shepherd who was healed at the grave of the murdered Tsarevich, he collapses. As bells toll, Boris falls dying, begging God for mercy. Shuiski and the other nobles place Boris's young son, Feodor, on the throne.

In the Kromy Forest, peasants attack a nobleman and two Jesuit priests. Gregory, hailed as Dmitri, passes by with his army, headed for Moscow. When all are gone, a simpleton is left on stage to lament Russia's fate.

(N.B. The two scenes of Act IV are sometimes played in the reverse order.)

Tchaikovsky

The Russian nationalism of The Five was opposed by Anton Rubinstein, the founder of the St. Petersburg Conservatory and a great champion of Western music. His most famous student was Tchaikovsky, whose music used western forms but infused them with Russian spirit and emotion.

Tchaikovsky's operatic output was relatively modest, but two of his works are still part of the standard repertoire.

OPPOSITE: **Two different productions of** *Pikovaya dama* **(***The Queen of Spades***), the first staged in Moscow in 2004 (top), the second a 2005 performance at the Festspielhaus in Baden-Baden, Germany, featuring Olga Guriakova as Lisa and Vladimir Galuzin as Herman (bottom).**

Tchaikovsky's early life and influences

Pyotr Ilyich Tchaikovsky's family moved to St. Petersburg in 1850 when he was ten years old. After passing his examinations at law school, he briefly became a civil servant before enrolling as one of the first students at the St. Petersburg Conservatory. He was such a brilliant student that he was soon engaged by Rubinstein's brother, Nicolai, as a professor at the Moscow Conservatory. He made little money from his music, however, and was resigned to a life of poverty when he met Nadezhda von Meck, a wealthy widow. She agreed to pay him a generous allowance on the condition that they never met and kept in touch by letter only. This rather strange relationship—which has never been satisfactorily explained—gave Tchaikovsky financial independence and he was able to resign his post at the conservatory.

Fame and tragedy

In 1877 Tchaikovsky embarked upon a disastrous marriage and the couple split up after only nine weeks. He tried to commit suicide by standing in an icy river. He was hoping to develop pneumonia, but only managed to catch a cold. As his music became

Eugene Onegin is Tchaikovsky's most famous opera and is widely staged to this day. This image features Mirella Freni and Nikolai Ghiaurov in an acclaimed 1986 production of this classic tale.

known throughout Europe, Tchaikovsky traveled more and more. In 1891, he visited the United States, where he was conductor at the official opening night of Carnegie Hall. Returning to Russia, he began work on what was to be his last symphony, "The Pathetique." Less than a week after conducting the symphony's premiere in St. Petersburg, Tchaikovsky drank a glass of unboiled water and contracted cholera. He died a few days later on November 6th, 1893.

Tchaikovsky's operas

Although he is best known in the West for his symphonies and ballet music, Tchaikovsky also wrote ten operas. Of these, two have entered the standard repertoire. *Yevgeny Onegin* (*Eugene Onegin*) (1878) is based on the poem by Pushkin. Its subject matter is distinctly Russian, but its theme, exploring the notion of destiny and the way in which lovers can become victims of social conventions, is universal.

Pikovaya dama (*Pique Dame* or *The Queen of Spades*) (1890) is also based on an original story by Pushkin, to a libretto by Tchaikovsky's brother, Modest. The main character of the opera, Herman, an army officer whose obsession with the "secret of the three cards" leads to his ruin and eventual death, is on stage throughout and sings in all seven scenes.

The mystery of Tchaikovsky's death

The accepted view that Tchaikovsky died of cholera has been challenged recently by a theory that he committed suicide by consuming small doses of arsenic, which would have led to symptoms similar to those of cholera. According to this theory, hotly disputed in Russia, he was being blackmailed over his homosexuality and was aided in his suicide by his brother, who was also homosexual. A short opera, *Shameful Vice*, which explores this version of events was written by Michael Finnissy, an English composer, in 1994.

Despite its origins in Russian literature, *Eugene Onegin*'s themes of love and destiny are universally understood and appreciated.

Czech opera

The modern Czech Republic consist of two distinct regions, Bohemia and Moravia. For much of their recent history, they formed part of the Austro-Hungarian Empire. Artistic life therefore tended to focus on Vienna rather than native tradition. This was to change during the 19th century, with the growth of nationalism.

Bedrich Smetana brought Czech opera to life, bravely using his native language to take stories of Slav peasant life to the European masses.

Smetana

Bedrich Smetana was to Czech opera what Glinka was to Russian. The son of a brewer, he was born in March, 1824. He studied music in Prague, despite opposition from his father, and, with financial help from Liszt, went on to establish his own music school. From 1857 onward he began consciously to compose music that reflected Bohemian national aspirations. His music used Czech dance rhythms and folk song melodies, while the stories of many of his operas were based on Czech peasant life. He also used the Czech language, which had only recently been granted official status by Austria. Tragically, by 1874 he had become deaf, an affliction compounded by tinnitus. In 1883, suffering from severe depression, he entered a mental hospital in Prague, where he died the following year.

Smetana's operas

Smetana's first opera in Czech was *Branibori v Cechách* (*The Brandenburgers in Bohemia*) (1863), a three-act opera based on an historical theme. It is rarely performed today, but his second opera, *Prodaná nevesta* (*The Bartered Bride*), was his masterpiece. There are four versions of this comic opera, varying between two and three acts. The final version was premiered in

Prague in 1870. In the later revisions, he added dance sequences, a chorus, and recitatives to replace the spoken passages. It was an assertion of pride in Czech language and traditions, but when it entered the international repertoire it was, until recently, generally performed in German. Smetana wrote six further operas, none of which achieved the same degree of success, but his place in the history of Czech music and his influence on later composers was assured.

The Bartered Bride exists in no fewer than four different versions. This comic opera is widely staged in many and varied incarnations.

Dvořák

Antonín Dvořák (1841–1904) is best known for his symphonic and chamber music rather than his operas. However, he actually wrote as many as ten, of which *Selma sedlák* (*The Cunning Peasant*) (1878) and *Rusalka* are the best known. The story of the latter is based on a Czech fairy tale about a water spirit (*rusalka* in Czech). First performed in Prague in 1901, it

Antonin Dvorák had an unusually internationalist outlook for a composer of his time, and this is reflected in much of his work. However, some of his ten operas were based on Czech fairy tales.

OPPOSITE: **The Australian tenor Stuart Skelton perfoming in the role of the Prince in Dvorák's most successful opera, *Rusalka*.**

was very popular in Czech lands but less so elsewhere. Like Tchaikovsky, Dvorák used his native roots in his music but was internationalist in his outlook. He also spent time in the United States, where he composed his best known work, the Symphony No 9, "From the New World." Upon arriving in the United States Dvorák prophetically remarked:

"I am convinced that the future music of this country must be founded on what are called Negro melodies. These can be the foundation of a serious and original school of composition, to be developed in the United States. These beautiful and varied themes are the product of the soil. They are the folk songs of America and your composers must turn to them."

Janácek

The greatest works of Leos Janácek, including *Sinfonietta* and the *Glagolitic Mass*, as well as four operas, were all written during the last decade of his life. Born in Moravia in 1854, he was largely self-taught but has come to be regarded as the greatest Czech operatic composer. He died in August 1928.

Leos Janácek matured late as a composer of opera, but this made his diverse tales of Slovak and Moravian life no less effective.

Janácek's operas

Following the success of his opera *Sárka* in 1881, Janácek began to make a systematic study of Moravian and Slovak folk music, especially its rhythms and vocal inflections. He incorporated this into his own music, most notably in the opera *Jenufa*, which he did not write until he was approaching fifty.

The subject matter of Janácek's operas is much darker than that of earlier Czech composers, in common with many other composers who produced operas in the years following the Great War. In *The Makropulos Affair* (1926) a cold and calculating woman seduces a young man and his father in order to obtain the formula for a potion that has kept her alive for over three hundred years. *Kátá Kabanová* (1921) ends with the suicide of its heroine, while *From the House of the Dead* (1928) is based on the novel by Dostoevsky. *Príhody Lisky Bystrousky (The Cunning Little Vixen)* (1924) is his lightest work, though even this ends with the vixen's death.

Despite his relatively advanced age and the serious tone of much of his work, Janacek was highly original and innovative in his writing. Although he based much of his work on folksong, the techniques he applied were often unorthodox.

Two scenes from a recent production of Janácek's *Jenufa*, the first
of which reflects the composer's interest in Slav music and culture
and the second the prevailing grimness of much of his work.

French opera

The popularity of Grand Opera was gradually replaced by *opéra comique*. This should not be translated as "comic opera." It refers to opera with spoken dialog, both lighthearted and serious.
The Opéra Comique was a theater that presented these works and which, after 1870, was less bound by tradition than the Paris Opéra.

Jakob Offenbach more or less single-handedly invented a new form of opera, *opéra bouffe*, most famously represented by *Orphée aux Enfers* (see below).

Offenbach

Jakob Offenbach was born in Cologne in 1819. His father, Isaac Juda Eberst, a cantor and violinist, adopted the name Offenbach as he was a native of Offenbach am Main. Jakob moved to Paris in 1833 to study the cello, changing his name to Jacques in the process, and took up a post in the orchestra of the Opéra Comique. He left France briefly in 1848, but in 1850 became the conductor at the Théâtre Français, before opening his own theater, the Bouffes Parisiens, in 1855. Here he became the undisputed master of *opéra bouffe*, a blend of music, dance, and witty spoken dialog.

Offenbach's best known work, *Orphée aux Enfers* (1858), is a boisterous parody of the more serious operatic treatments of this love story. The gallop from this operetta is the music most frequently associated with the can-can and widely regarded as being quintessentially French. His other works include *La Belle Hélène* (1864) and *La Vie Parisienne* (1866). His final opera, unfinished at his death in 1880, was *Les Contes d'Hoffmann* (*The Tales of Hoffmann*), a much more serious work dealing with the conflict between art and love.

The Tales of Hoffmann demonstrated the more serious side of Offenbach's talent and, although it was unfinished at his death, is widely performed today.

Orientalism

Toward the end of the 19th century, as Western European countries expanded their colonial empires, there was a fashionable interest in the West for all things oriental. This fascination is revealed in a number of French operas. These include Delibes' *Lakmé*, first performed at the Opéra Comique in 1883. It is the story of a Hindu girl who falls in love with a British soldier. To avoid conflict between her lover and her father, Lakmé commits suicide. The opera is best known for the Flower Duet in Act 1, widely used in a famous airline commercial. Bizet's *Les Pêcheurs de Perles* (*The Pearl Fishers*) (1863) is set in Ceylon, while Massenet's *Le Roi de Lahore* (*The King of Lahore*) (1877) has an Indian setting. Debussy's interest in music from other cultures, particularly that of Java, influenced his only opera, *Pelléas et Mélisande* (1893–1902), the simplicity and understatement of which marked a turning point in music.

The Canadian tenor Stuart
Howe playing Gérald in a 2003
production of Delibes' *Lakmé*
(also pictured on page 94).

OPPOSITE: **The baritone Adam
Flowers performing the lead role
in a recent production of Bizet's
The Pearl Fishers.**

Bizet's Carmen

Undoubtedly the best known French opera of this period, Bizet's *Carmen* (1875) was a critical failure at first. Some found that there was too much spoken dialog, while others denounced the subject matter as "immoral" and "superficial." Bizet died three months after its premiere, unaware of the fame it would soon enjoy.

Although he wrote many and diverse other operas, it is the universally popular Carmen for which Georges Bizet is remembered.

Bizet

Parisian by birth, Georges Bizet spent his entire life in the city, apart from a few years in Rome, from his birth in 1838 to his death a mere 36 years later. A child prodigy, he began studying at the Paris Conservatory when he was only ten years old. In 1857 he shared a prize for his setting of the one-act opera *Le Docteur Miracle* and, the same year, commenced his stay in Italy as winner of the Prix de Rome. The opera buffa, *Don Procopio*, written in Rome, was not performed until 1906. Another opera written under the terms of the Prix de Rome, *La Guzla de L'Emir*, was rehearsed at the Opéra-Comique, but was withdrawn when Bizet was invited to compose *Les Pêcheurs de Perles* (*The Pearl Fishers*) for the Théâtre-Lyrique. Shortly after this, Bizet also wrote the opera *La Jolie Fille de Perth* and the romantic opera *Djamileh*. *Carmen* had its premiere at the Opéra Comique on March 3rd, 1875, but Bizet died only months later on his sixth wedding anniversary. He is buried at Père Lachaise Cemetery in Paris.

The appeal of Carmen

The story centers on a beautiful but fiery gypsy who works at the Seville cigarette factory. She uses her charms to persuade the corporal Don José to disobey his superior. Infatuated with her, he joins the gang of smugglers of which she is a member. After a brief period of happiness, she rejects him for the bullfighter Escamillo and he stabs her to death. *Carmen* is notable for its realism and for the way that it does not turn away from the more unsavory aspects of ordinary life. This sense of realism was brought to its full realization, however, in Italy, with the development of the style known as *Verismo*.

Carmen features some of the best-loved arias and melodies in the entire repertoire of opera, as well as telling a thoroughly gripping and entertaining tale.

Carmen

One of the most frequently staged of all operas, Bizet's *Carmen* deals with passion and murder on a domestic scale. Following its disappointing premiere in 1875, it has captured the popular imagination like no other opera, spawning several film versions and numerous ballet versions.

Act I

In a square in Seville, soldiers idle outside a cigarette factory. Micaëla appears, seeking José, her fiancé, but leaves when the soldiers flirt with her. José enters with the new guard and the female workers emerge from the cigarette factory to be greeted by a group of young men. Among the women is Carmen, obviously a great favorite. When asked to choose a lover, she throws a flower to José, who tries to ignore her. Later, a fight breaks out and Carmen slashes the face of another woman. Don José's superior, Captain

Bizet's story of passion, intrigue, and betrayal has enthralled audiences worldwide for over a century with a series of memorable melodies and arias.

Zuniga, orders him to escort her to jail. On the way, she seduces him and he lets her escape, for which he is arrested.

Act II

At an inn with her smuggler friends, Carmen is wooed by both Captain Zuniga and the toreador, Escamillo, but she can only think of José. Finally, José arrives, having served his prison sentence. Carmen dances for him but is interrupted by the trumpets calling the soldiers to the barracks. Her temper flares when he makes to leave, causing him to pledge his devotion to her. She says he must join the smugglers if he really loves her. He refuses and is about to go when he is surprised by Zuniga. After a brief stand-off, he flees with Carmen.

Act III

José arrives at a rocky gorge with the smugglers, but Carmen has now turned her affections to Escamillo. A fight between José and Escamillo over Carmen is narrowly averted by the smugglers. Micaëla appears and tells José that his dying mother wishes to see him. Vowing that he will return to Carmen, he leaves. As he is leaving, Escamillo is heard singing in the distance and Carmen rushes to him.

Act IV

Outside the bullring, Carmen promises herself to Escamillo if he returns victorious. Before she can enter the arena, however, she is confronted by José . When she throws back his ring, he stabs her. As she dies, Escamillo triumphs in the arena. The spectators exit as José confesses his action to all.

Verismo

Verismo (Italian for "realism") initially referred to a movement in Italian literature. Exponents of verismo—the *veristi*—were particularly interested in the life of the lower classes, life in the southern regions of Italy and local customs. Veristic plays were called *scene populari* and served as the basis for many of the verismo operas.

must know

Originally, *Verismo* was an Italian literary movement which originated between 1875 and 1895. It was mainly inspired by French naturalism, but unlike that movement, which was based on positivistic ideals, verismo was essentially pessimistic, based on the premise of "impersonality," meaning that the writer should not impose any personal meaning or point of view to his works.

"Cav and Pag"

The first two great verismo operas were Mascagni's *Cavalleria Rusticana* (*Rustic Chivalry*) (1890) and *Pagliacci*, written in 1892 by Leoncavallo. The former is a tale of passion and betrayal in a small Sicilian town, ending in a duel with knives. The latter tells a story of love, jealousy, and murder amongst a band of touring clowns, ending with the famous line *"La commedia è finita"* (The Show Is Over). *Pagliacci* was actually based on real-life incidents reported in contemporary newspapers. Both operas are short in length—at only just over an hour each—and are traditionally performed together as a double bill.

The clown characters and comic look of Leoncavallo's *Pagliacci* belie a gritty storyline based on real events which is typical of the realistic verismo style.

Mascagni's *Cavalleria Rusticana* was first performed in 1890, but is often staged today in a wide variety of updated styles.

Other verismo composers

Other composers working in the verismo style included Francesco Cilea (1866–1950), whose best known work is *Adriana Lecouvreur* (1902), and Umberto Giordano (1867–1948), who wrote *Andrea Chénier* in 1896. The best known of all Italian composers during this period, however, was Giacomo Puccini, whose operas combined verismo with an interest in exotic locations. Puccini's operas are also notable for the powerful and sympathetic roles he created for his women characters.

Puccini

In 1880, Puccini completed a setting of the Catholic mass, which provides an idea of the operas that were to come. The *Messa*, with its powerful arias and stirring choruses, is very operatic. His *Preludio Sinfonico*, composed two years later, shows his gift for melody.

Puccini took up Verdi's mantle in the late 19th century and became the new standard-bearer of popular Italian opera.

Puccini's early career

After studying music with his uncle, Fortunato Magi, Puccini started his career at the age of 14 as an organist at St. Martino and St. Michele in his home town of Lucca in 1872. After seeing a performance of Verdi's *Aïda* in Pisa, however, he decided that his future was in opera. From 1880 until 1883, he studied in Milan and in 1882 entered a competition for a one-act opera. Although he did not win, his entry, *Le Villi*, did bring him public attention. *Manon Lescaut* (1893), his third opera, was a great success, launching a partnership with librettist, Luigi Illica, that saw the creation of *La Bohème* (1896), *Tosca* (1900), and *Madame Butterfly* (1904). These ultimately confirmed his status as one of the most popular composers in the history of opera.

La Bohème is widely considered to be Puccini's masterpiece, but with its mixture of lighthearted and sentimental scenes and its largely conversational style it was not a success when it was first staged in Turin in 1896. *Tosca*, Puccini's first excursion into verismo, was more enthusiastically received by the Roman audience at the Teatro Costanzi, and this success drove Puccini onto even more ambitious plans.

In 1900, soon after the first production of *Tosca*, Puccini visited London and saw David Belasco's

one-act play *Madame Butterfly*. This he took as the basis for his next collaboration with Illica and Giacosa, the librettists who had worked on *La Bohème* and *Tosca*; he considered it the best and technically most advanced opera he had written.

Scandal and success

In 1909, Puccini was involved in a scandal that could have formed the story for an opera. His wife, Elvira, wrongly accused their maid, Doria Manfredi, of having an affair with Puccini, following which the maid commited suicide. Her family sued Elvira and Puccini had to pay damages. In 1910, Puccini completed a commission for the New York Metropolitan Opera, *La Fanciulla del West* (*The Girl of the Golden West*). A story of love and betrayal in the old west, its main character is Minnie, the hard-talking owner of a Californian poker saloon. The world premiere was conducted by Arturo Toscanini, who had done much to develop American interest in Italian opera, particularly in verismo operas.

It was Toscanini who conducted the first performance of Puccini's last opera, *Turandot*, at La Scala in 1926. Puccini, a chronic chain smoker, had died of throat cancer in 1924 before completing the opera. It was completed by another composer, Franco Alfano, but at the premiere, Toscanini stopped the perfomance at the last point that Puccini himself had completed and orchestrated. The performers froze in position, whileToscanini turned to the audience and said:

"Here the opera finishes, because here the Maestro laid down his pen."

Madame Butterfly

Following the resounding successes of *Manon Lescaut*, *La Bohème*, and *Tosca*, everyone expected another triumph for Puccini, but the opening night of *Madame Butterfly* in February, 1904, was a disaster. The score was revised, with the long second act being divided into two. Less than four months later, the opera opened again and this time was a great success.

Act I

The opera opens in Nagasaki at the turn of the century. A Japanese broker, Goro, has arranged a marriage for an American naval officer, Lieutenant Pinkerton, with Cio-San (Madame Butterfly). The contract has a convenient let-out clause, which allows the marriage to be canceled at a month's notice. Cio-San, who is only fifteen, makes her entrance and tells Pinkerton about herself and her family. The wedding, however, is interrupted by Bonze, her uncle, who turns her relatives against her because she has chosen to adopt Christianity. Pinkerton orders everyone away and together he and Cio-San enter their new home.

Act II

Three years later, Pinkerton has disappeared. Suzuki, Cio-San's servant, warns her that he will never return, though her warnings are ignored. Sharpless, the American consul, arrives with a letter, telling of Pinkerton's marriage to an American girl, but he does not have the heart to break the news. He does, however, advise Cio-San to accept an offer of marriage from Prince Yamadori. Cio-San insists that this is

impossible, as she has a son by Pinkerton. A cannon is heard from the harbor, announcing the arrival of Pinkerton's ship, the *Abraham Lincoln*. Joyfully, Cio-San and Suzuki await the arrival of its captain.

A scene from a 1990s production of *Madame Butterfly*. Robynne Redmon stars as Suzuki (left), and Nikki Li Hartliep as Cio-Cio-San.

Act III

Into Cio-San's garden comes Sharpless, accompanied by Pinkerton and his new bride, Kate. Pinkerton cannot bear to face his former wife and leaves, after singing a passionate farewell. Cio-San enters and, seeing Kate Pinkerton, realizes what has happened. Left alone with her child, she blindfolds him then goes behind a screen and stabs herself with her father's dagger. As she crawls toward her son, Pinkerton enters and falls to his knees beside her body.

Opera in Spain

So far, no mention has been made of opera in Spain. In fact, a separate, specifically Spanish style, called *zarzuela*, had followed its own course there since the 17th century. Zarzuela is a genre that alternates between spoken and sung scenes, the latter incorporating elaborate dances with multiple performers.

Zarzuela

The name probably comes from a hunting lodge, the Palacio de la Zarzuela near Madrid, where, in the 17th century, this type of performance first took place before the Spanish royal court. Zarzuela can be divided into two main forms, Baroque Zarzuela, the earliest style, and Romantic Zarzuela, which developed in the 19th century. During the period of Spanish colonization, zarzuela was taken to the Phillipines and Cuba, where it absorbed the influences of local music.

Early zarzuela

The first performance of what came to be called zarzuela took place in 1657, when the court of King Philip IV was entertained by a new comedy, *Laurel de Apolo*, written by Pedro Calderón de la Barca, with music by Juan de Hidalgo. This new genre matched witty libretti with music that ranged from operatic arias and choruses to popular songs. It is this incorporation of popular songs and dances that makes zarzuela distinctive. The growing popularity of Italian opera during the 18th century, however, made the home-grown style less fashionable and it developed into shorter forms, *tonadilla* and *sainette*, which were the equivalent of the Italian *intermezzi*. The poet Ramón de la Cruz was the writer of

must know

Francisco Asenjo Barbieri (1823–1894) was the most influential Spanish composer of the 19th century. He studied clarinet, piano, and singing at the Madrid Conservatory. His first opera, *Il Buontempone* (1847) was in Italian, but in 1850, he produced his first zarzuela.

libretti that reflected everyday life and speech, rather than the mythological stories that had been the mainstay of zarzuela until then.

The golden age of zarzuela

The late 19th century was the golden age of zarzuela. Romantic zarzuela was an exotic mixture of musical and dramatic styles. It combined elegant arias and musical interludes with dialog (both in verse and prose), popular songs, and vulgar comedy. The longer examples were referred to as *género grande*, but more popular were the short one-act *género chico*, which often had their location in the more dubious areas of Madrid. The greatest zarzuela grande was *El Barberillo de Lavapiés* by Francisco Barbieri, while his pupil, Federico Chueca, was the master of zarzuela chico.

Spanish opera in the 20th century

Although zarzuela continued to flourish in the early years of the 20th century, the Spanish Civil War brought about its decline. Noteworthy composers of latter-day zarzuela were Amadeo Vives (*Doña Francisquita*, 1923) and Federico Moreno Torroba (*Luisa Fernanda*, 1932). The classic repertoire has been kept alive mainly through recordings made from the 1950s onward. A new form of entertainment, known as *revistas* (or reviews) grew from zarzuela. These works were much shorter and often had sexual themes, with great use of double entendres. The songs from these revistas became a part of Spanish popular culture. Meanwhile, in the former Spanish colonies, a more politically aware form of zarzuela developed, often dealing with the situation of the black and mixed-race underclass in these societies.

Popular songs (above) and traditional Spanish dancing (below) combine to create the unique operatic form that is zarzuela.

Operas and language

During the 19th century the struggle to maintain or revive local languages became part of the struggle for national identity. A number of operas were written in some of the less widely spoken European languages, including Finnish and Welsh, as an expression of this growing nationalism.

Finland

During the 19th century, Finland was part of the Russian Empire, but there was a growing sense of national identity, most notably expressed in music by the composer Jean Sibelius (1865–1957). In 1898, the Finnish Literature Society organized a competition for an opera in Finnish, based on the national epic, the *Kalevala*. The result was the first Finnish language opera, *Pohjan Neiti* (*Maiden of the North*) by Oskar Merikanto (1868–1924). This was followed in 1909 by a second Kalevala opera, *Aino*, by Erkki Melartin (1875–1937). More recently composers Aulis Sallinen (*The Red Line*) and Kaija Saariaho (*L'Amour de loin*) have attracted worldwide attention.

Wales

The opera *Blodwen* (1878) was the first opera in the Welsh language. It did very well initially, receiving some 500 performances, but has since fallen into obscurity. It was written by Joseph Parry, who was born in the Welsh industrial town of Merthyr Tydfil in 1841. Parry began work as a coal miner at the age of nine. The family emigrated to the United States in 1854, settling in a Welsh community in Pennsylvania. Joseph worked in an iron works but

OPPOSITE: **Joseph Parry (1841–1903), the composer of the first Welsh language opera, *Blodwen*.**

also studied music, setting Welsh texts to music and performing widely both in America and in Wales. He returned to Britain to study music in London and Cambridge. He wrote nine other operas besides *Blodwen*, but is best remembered now for the hymn tune Aberystwyth and the famous Welsh love song "Myfanwy." He died in Cardiff in 1903.

want to know more?

For a flavor of the national styles that developed during the 19th century, try these CDs:

- *The Glory of Russian Opera* A three-disc boxed set available in the US only. Russian Season:B00000HXHQ
- *Scenes From Operas on the Subjects by Pushkin* Boheme (US): B00004WH86 BMR (UK):B00004WH86
- Smetana—*The Bartered Bride* Chandos:B000BLI370
- Offenbach—*Orpheus In The Underworld/La Vie Parisienne/La Belle Hélène* (Highlights in English) Angel Records (US):B00009KHY3 Classics for Pleasure(UK): B00009KHY3
- Puccini—*Opera Highlights Various Artists* A five-disc boxed set only available in the UK or online. Emi Classics: B000067FH2
- *Zarzuela: Spanish Operetta* A three-disc, budget-priced boxed set. Brilliant Classics: B0002VOXNW

8 Opera in the 20th century

The 20th century was a period of enormous international upheaval, combined with improvements in technology on a scale never seen before in history. In terms of music, however, it would be a mistake to see the century as a complete break with the past. National styles continued to develop, but there was also a growing internationalism, as interest in atonal and serial music spread. In addition to folk music, composers now began to incorporate influences from jazz into their work.

The influence of Wagner

During his lifetime and in the years that followed, Wagner inspired almost fanatical devotion in his supporters. Even those who opposed him, such as Debussy, recognized that his work had broken important new ground, leading to the development of what is still referred to, over one hundred years later, as "modern music."

Richard Strauss's operatic output was prolific and multi-faceted, with influences ranging from Wagner to the Bible and Freud.

OPPOSITE: *Salome* was typical of Strauss's early work. This one-act opera was based on the Oscar Wilde play, which in turn was derived from the New Testament tale of King Herod's step-daughter, who demanded the head of John the Baptist.

Richard Strauss

Strauss was the dominant figure in early 20th century German opera. As the influence of Romanticism faded, new movements developed— impressionism, expressionism, and orientalism. Strauss incorporated all of these into his work. He was also heavily influenced by the new theories concerning human emotions put forward by Sigmund Freud. His operas fall into two categories. The first, dealing with mythic figures from the Bible and classical sources, incorporated musical ideas that many found difficult and even shocking. The second, however, was nostalgic, evoking a lost golden era of Austro-Germanic culture.

Strauss's start in music

Strauss' father, who gave the composer his first musical education, was the principal horn player at the Munich court opera. He started writing his own music at the age of six. In 1874, at the age of ten, he heard Wagner's music for the first time and it was to have an enormous influence upon him. His father disapproved, however, and it was not until six years later that he was finally able to obtain and study the score of *Tristan und Isolde*. In 1832, he entered

must know

A tone poem is a piece of orchestral music based on a poem, painting, landscape, or other non-musical source. Examples include *Don Quixote* by Richard Strauss, Smetana's *Má Vlast*, a series of six tone poems depicting his native country, and Tchaikovsky's *Romeo and Juliet* overture.

OPPOSITE: *Elektra* (top), like *Salome*, provoked extreme audience reactions. It was based on a Greek tragedy and was unremittingly gloomy. *Der Rosenkavalier* (bottom) was altogether more frivolous.

Munich University, where he studied philosophy and art history rather than music. After university he secured a post as assistant conductor to Hans von Bülow in Munich. In September, 1894, he married the soprano Pauline Maria de Ahna and, despite her reputation for being bossy and bad-tempered, their marriage was long and happy. His early music had been rather conservative, but this was to change when he met the composer and violinist, Alexander Ritter, who introduced him to the essays of Wagner and persuaded him to start writing his tone poems.

The Strauss operas

After two early critical failures (*Guntram* in 1894 and *Feuersnot* in 1901), Strauss wrote *Salome* in 1905 (pictured on page 134). Based on the play by Oscar Wilde, it received extreme audience reactions, partly because of its subject matter, which involves incest and necrophilia, but also for his use of dissonance in the music. The public outcry in New York was so great that it closed after just one performance at the Metropolitan Opera. His next opera, *Elektra* (1909) was even more discordant. *Elektra* was followed, in 1910, by a very different opera, *Der Rosenkavalier* (*The Knight*

Der Rosenkavalier is a comic opera in three acts adapted from the novel *Les amours du chevalier de Faublas* by Louvet de Couvrai and Molière's comedy *Monsieur de Pourceaugnac*.

Ariadne auf Naxos was first performed at the Hoftheater, Stuttgart, on October 25th, 1912. It is mainly a reworking of the Greek myth of Ariadne and Bacchus.

of the Rose). Its story of a romance between a seventeen-year-old youth and a thirty-two-year-old woman is accompanied by music that is full of waltzes and bitter-sweet melodies. Strauss continued to write operas regularly until 1940. These included *Ariadne auf Naxos* (1912), *Intermezzo* (1923), *Arabella* (1932), and *Capriccio* (1941). After the impact of his first operas, Strauss' harmonic and melodic language was looking rather old-fashioned by this time. In 1947, he famously said of himself, *"I may not be a first-rate composer, but I am a first-class second-rate composer."* He died, at the age of 85, in 1949.

Strauss and the Nazis

There is controversy over the role Strauss played after the Nazi party came to power. In November 1933 Goebbels appointed him to the post of president of the *Reichsmusikkammer*, the State Music Bureau. Although he was not consulted about this appointment, Strauss decided to keep his post, which has been seen by some as evidence of Nazi sympathies. On the other hand, his decision to write the one-act opera *Friedenstag* in 1938 was certainly courageous. Set in a beseiged fortress during the Thirty Years' War, it is a thinly-veiled criticism of the Nazi regime.

OPPOSITE: *Ariadne auf Naxos* recounts the strife-torn lovelife of the eponymous heroine. Ariadne is abandoned on Naxos by Theseus, but is then swept off her feet by Bacchus, who promises to set her in the heavens as a constellation.

Atonality and serialism

A feature of music since the late 19th century, and especially since the end of the First World War, has been the move away from the traditional notions of tonality that have dominated Western music. The Austrians Arnold Schoenberg and Alban Berg had a great influence on other composers.

Schoenberg's work was characterized by an entirely new approach, in that much of it was completely *atonal* (see below).

Schoenberg

Arnold Franz Walter Schönberg was born in Vienna in September 1874. (He officially changed the spelling of his surname when he left Germany in 1933.) He was largely self-taught as a musician, but his early compositions were much admired by both Richard Strauss and Gustav Mahler. During the summer of 1908, Schoenberg wrote *Du lehnest wider eine Silberweide* (*You lean against a silver willow*), his first composition with no recognizable key. This was followed in 1912 by one of his most influential works, *Pierrot Lunaire*. This was a cycle of songs utilizing a technique known as *sprechstimme* (speak-singing) for a female singer (dressed in a pierrot costume) accompanied by a small ensemble of musicians. He went on to create the dodecaphonic (or twelve-tone) method of composition.

Moses und Aron

Between 1930 and 1932, Schoenberg worked on his opera *Moses und Aron*. He wrote over two thirds of the opera but was never able to complete it, the music ending at the point where Moses cries out in frustration that he cannot express himself. The opera, composed using the dodecaphonic system, is much more than just a retelling of the Biblical story of Moses and Aaron. It is an exploration of the different kinds of leadership they can offer the Jewish people. In 1933, Schoenberg reconverted to Judaism, having become a Lutheran as a young man. Although a great influence on other composers, his music was not acceptable to the Nazis and he was forced into exile in 1933, moving first to Paris and then to the United States, where he died in 1951.

Berg

Alban Berg did not show any interest in music until his late teens. Born in Vienna in 1885, he started studying with Schoenberg in 1904 and remained his student for six years. From 1915–1918 he served in the Austrian army, and it was during this period that he started work on his first opera, *Wozzeck*. Completed in 1922, it was not performed in its full version until 1925. A second opera, *Lulu*, was composed in 1935, but was left with its third act unfinished at his death, from blood poisoning caused by an insect bite.

Berg's operas

Wozzeck and *Lulu* both reflect the mood of the shattered societies of post-war Germany and Austria. Wozzeck, feeling abused by both society and his mistress, murders her then accidentally drowns himself. The main character in *Lulu* makes her way in society through a series of sexual relationships, with both men and women, then descends into prostitution and eventual death at the hands of Jack the Ripper. Berg wrote his own libretti, based on the plays of Georg Büchner and Frank Wedekind. The music adapts Schoenberg's twelve-tone theory in a highly personal way, using elements of tonal and atonal music and snatches of popular songs.

must know

"Serialism" refers to the compositional technique developed by Schoenberg and others in which notes are arranged in a sequence with each note appearing only once. This is the "tone row" from which the rest of the composition is built.

Berg's *Wozzeck* is a thoroughly gloomy tale. The disturbed anti-hero in the title role murders his mistress and then kills himself unintentionally in a fit of panic (see pages 144-5).

Wozzeck

Berg's opera was first performed in Berlin in 1925, a period when old ideas and values were breaking down. This was the time of Freud and Kafka and also the rise of National Socialism, an era of intellectual revolution but also of social and moral decay.

Act I

The simple soldier, Wozzeck, is shaving his Captain, and complaining that poverty makes it difficult to be virtuous. Later, when Wozzeck and his companion are working in the fields, he has frightening visions. The scene shifts to the room of Marie, Wozzeck's mistress, where she is looking at a military parade passing by. Wozzeck comes along and tells Marie of his terrible premonitions. The regimental doctor, an amateur psychologist, convinces Wozzeck that he may be going mad. In the final scene, Marie talks with the Drum-major outside her room. After a brief flirtation, she yields to his advances.

Act II

Marie is admiring the earrings the Drum-major gave her. Wozzeck arrives and when he asks where she got them she says she found them. Though not convinced, Wozzeck feels sorry for her child and gives her money. Later, in the street, the Doctor and the Captain meet Wozzeck and hint that Marie is being unfaithful. Wozzeck confronts her and is about to hit her, when she says "better a knife in my belly than your hands on me." Later, he sees her dancing with the Drum-major. In a scene full of confused events, Wozzeck feels that he is losing his mind. In

must know

Sigmund Freud (1856–1939) was an Austrian psychologist best known for his studies of sexual desire, repression, and the power of the subconscious.

Franz Kafka (1883–1924) was born in Prague, the child of a German-speaking Jewish family. His novels and short stories portray a world that seems random and absurd, its characters often victims of a faceless bureaucracy.

the barracks that night he talks in his sleep about a knife-blade. The Drum-major comes in, drunk, and Wozzeck attacks him, but is badly beaten.

Act III

Marie asks God for forgiveness. That night, she and Wozzeck are walking near a pond. He talks earnestly of love, then draws out a knife and plunges it into her throat. He rushes to an inn, where he dances with Marget, Marie's neighbor. As he flirts with her, she notices blood on his hands and Wozzeck rushes out. He returns to the murder scene to find the blood-stained knife. He throws it into the pond, but then wades in to retrieve it. In his panic, he stumbles, falls and drowns. The next morning, children are playing outside Marie's house. Hearing the news that her body has been found, they rush off—all except Marie's child, who continues playing.

Neo-classicism

The rational, almost mathematical, approach to composition that defines serial music can be seen as a reaction against the excesses of Romanticism and Nationalism that made the carnage of the First World War possible. Another reaction was a return to the balance and restraint of 18th century classicism—a style known as neo-classicism.

Stravinsky's music provoked strong reactions. The complex music and violent dance steps of *The Rite of Spring* **so upset the Parisian audience at its debut that a riot took place.**

Stravinsky

Igor Stravinsky is most famous for his ballet music, but he also produced four operas, adopting a neo-classical style. The earliest of these is *Mavra*, premiered in Paris in 1922. A one-act opera buffa, based on Pushkin's poem *A Cottage in Kolomna*, it parodies the Russian-Italian style of the early 19th century. *Oedipus Rex* was written in Nice between January 1926 and March 1927. Its subject is taken from Greek mythology, with a libretto (by Jean Cocteau) translated into Latin. Stravinsky wanted the opera presented with minimal stage action. He envisaged the chorus sitting in a row with their faces concealed, while the solo singers stood on elevated platforms at different heights to each other. His fairy-tale opera *La Rossignol* is often paired with *Oedipus Rex*.

The Rake's Progress

The most widely performed of Stravinsky's operas is *The Rake's Progress*. First performed in Venice in 1951, it is based on the famous series of engravings by William Hogarth and has a libretto by W. H. Auden and Chester Kallman. The opera is styled on

Two scenes from Stravinsky's *The Rake's Progress*. This production from the year 2000 featured a set design by the California-based British artist David Hockney.

the music of Mozart and Rossini, and has recitatives (with harpsichord accompaniment), arias, and all the other traditional features of 18th and early 19th century opera, but the harmony and orchestration are unmistakably Stravinsky. Although criticized by some as being derivative, it has become part of the standard repertoire. The British artist David Hockney has also created stage designs for the Stravinsky opera.

Jazz and popular music

The reaction against Romanticism, and what were seen as the excesses of Wagner, was particularly strong in France. One way in which this was expressed was in the deliberate use of popular music and jazz influences by composers such as Ravel and Poulenc. In Germany, meanwhile, Kurt Weill produced stage music that owed much to cabaret.

must know

Alongside Debussy, Ravel was the defining composer of the Impressionist movement. He was renowned for his glittering, sensuous use of the orchestra, and his virtuoso piano writing. His best-known work is *Boléro*, which he described as *"a piece for orchestra without music."*

Ravel

Joseph-Maurice Ravel (1875–1937) is best known to the general public for his orchestration of Mussorgsky's *Pictures at an Exhibition*, the ballet *Daphnis et Chloé* and his orchestral work *Boléro*. He was influenced by Spanish, Gypsy, and Basque rhythms and melodies and in the 1920s he also developed an interest in jazz

A contemporary Dutch production of Ravel's opera *L'enfant et les Sortilèges* (*The Child and the Enchantments*), one of only two that he produced.

and blues. He produced two operas, *L'Heure Espagnole* (*The Spanish Hour*) (1911) and *L'enfant et les Sortilèges* (*The Child and the Enchantments*) (1925). The first of these, a one-act comic opera, displays the strong Spanish influence present in much of his music. The second is a children's opera in which a naughty child is punished when furniture and animals assume personalities of their own.

Poulenc

Francis Jean Marcel Poulenc was born in Paris in 1899. After the First World War, he became involved with a group of young French composers, referred to as *Les Six*, whose music was deliberately vulgar and anti-Romantic, using elements from popular song and the music-hall. Poulenc had considerable success with his comic opera *Les Mamelles de Tiresias* (*The Breasts of*

must know

Erik Satie (1866–1925) is best known for his piano music, which is humorous, minimalist, and often has bizarre instructions for the performer. He also wrote extensively for the stage. In 1917, the first performance of the ballet *Parade*, the score of which includes a ship's foghorn and a typewriter, caused a scandal. Satie was a great influence on the French avant-garde.

Poulenc's very accessible style of opera has always been well received. This a scene from a recent production of *Les Mamelles de Tiresias* (*The Breasts of Tiresias*).

must know

Les Six is the name used to unite the composers Poulenc, Milhaud, Auric, Durey, Honegger, and Tailleferre, though, in fact, their actual music has little in common. They had links with Jean Cocteau and Eric Satie and were united in their distaste for late Romanticism.

Tiresias) in 1947. It was based on Apollinaire's surrealist play, written in 1917.The story is set in Zanzibar, an imaginary town on the French Riviera, and its heroine is Thérèse, a feminist. In the first act, her breasts, a pair of balloons, escape and float upwards, while she starts to grow a beard. In contrast, the tragic opera *Les Dialogues des Carmélites* (1957) deals with the execution of Carmelite nuns during the French Revolution. Poulenc's final opera, a one-act tragedy by Jean Cocteau called *La Voix Humaine* (*The Human Voice*) was premiered at the Paris Opéra Comique in February 1959. Poulenc died of heart failure, in Paris, on 30 January 1963.

Kurt Weill

Although he had some success with his early instrumental works (which included a string quartet, a suite for orchestra, and his first symphony) Weill moved more and more toward vocal music, and especially toward writing for the stage. In his twenties, he met the singer Lotte Lenya and married her twice, first in 1926 and again, after their divorce in 1933, in 1937. She was a great interpreter of his work and, after his death in 1950, established the Kurt Weill Foundation to increase awareness of his music. Weill left Nazi Germany in 1933, settling first in Paris and emigrating to the United States in 1935. He became a naturalized American citizen in 1943.

A contemporary poster for Weill's *The Threepenny Opera* reflects the edginess and darkness of much of Weill's writing. This work was not a critical success.

Weill's operas

Weill's best known opera is *Die Dreigroschenoper* (*The Threepenny Opera*). Produced in partnership with the playwright Bertolt Brecht, it is a reworking of John Gay's *The Beggar's Opera*. It contains Weill's most

A German-born Jew, Weill left his native country in 1933 at the start of the Nazi regime and settled in America, where his work received mixed reactions.

famous song, "*Die Moritat von Mackie Messer*" (*Mack the Knife*). *Happy End*, a second collaboration with Brecht, opened on September 2nd, 1929 but closed after only seven performances. The opening night of *Aufstieg und Fall der Stadt Mahagonny* (*Rise and Fall of the City of Mahogany*), which includes the famous "Alabama Song," was unable to continue because of a riot organized by members of the Nazi party. Weill, as a Jew and a collaborator with Brecht, a Communist, was forced to leave Germany. In America, he continued to produce works for the stage, and his productions for Broadway, including *Lady in the Dark* and *Love Life*, contributed to the development of the American musical. His major operatic success in America was *Street Scene*.

must know

Mack the Knife was a character based on the dashing highwayman Macheath in John Gay's *The Beggar's Opera*. The Brecht-Weill version was less dashing and much more cruel and sinister and has been transformed into a modern anti-hero.

Opera and totalitarianism

A number of the composers written about so far fell foul of the authorities in Nazi Germany. Official opposition to new music was not confined to Germany, however, and the Soviet Union under Stalin was also a dangerous place to produce music that did not meet with state approval.

Prokofiev's musical career was hindered by the oppressive Communist regime under which he lived and worked. Much of his work was subject to compulsory revisions.

Prokofiev

In 1904, at the age of thirteen, Sergei Sergeyevich Prokofiev moved from his birthplace in Ukraine to St. Petersburg, where, considerably younger than the other students, he studied at the conservatory. In 1917, he composed his Classical Symphony and an opera based on Dostoyevsky's novel *The Gambler*. Rehearsals for the latter were beset with problems and the premiere had to be canceled because of the February Revolution. Following the October Bolshevik Revolution, Prokofiev decided to leave Russia. He settled first in San Francisco, where he began work on his opera *Love for Three Oranges*, but in 1920 moved to Paris. By the early 1930s Prokofiev was starting to long for Russia again. His music was meeting with more success there. *Lieutenant Kije* was commissioned as the score to a Russian film and another commission, from the Kirov Theater in Leningrad, was the ballet *Romeo and Juliet*. In 1934, Prokofiev returned to Russia permanently.

A composer in the Soviet Union

At this time in the Soviet Union, a special bureau, the "Composers' Union," was established in order to regulate what was acceptable for composers to write. The worst crime was to be accused of "formalism," a vaguely defined term that could be used to prevent any kind of musical experimentation. Prokofiev described it as referring to *"Music that isn't understood on its first hearing."* He had successes with his ballet music and with the children's work *Peter and the Wolf*, but he was less successful with his operas. The premiere of *Semyon Kotko* (1940), about a hero of the Russian Revolution, was postponed because the producer, Vsevolod Meyerhold, was imprisoned and executed. The opera did not finally enter the repertoire of the Bolshoi Theater until 1970.

War and Peace

The German invasion of the Soviet Union and the start of The Great Patriotic War inspired Prokofiev to start work on *Vojna i mir* (*War and Peace*). It is a huge opera, with thirteen scenes. In the tradition of Mussorgsky, it makes extensive use of the chorus. The Composers' Union, however, insisted on numerous changes and revisions to the opera and Prokofiev was forced to pad it out with patriotic choruses. At the end of the war, the composer was accused of "formalism" in his music and in February 1948, his wife, Lina, was arrested for "espionage." His opera projects were quickly canceled at the Kirov Theater and, his health declining, Prokofiev withdrew from public life. His last performance was the premiere of his Seventh Symphony in 1952. He died of a cerebral haemorrage on March 5th, 1953, ironically on the same day as Stalin. The complete version of *War and Peace* did not finally receive its first performance until 1955.

must know

War and Peace— Tolstoy's monumental novel, telling the story of Russian society during the period of the Napoleonic wars— was first published from 1865 to 1869.

Untouchable genius

Although he is best known for his symphonies and string quartets, Shostakovich also produced two operas, the second of which led to a period of official condemnation that persuaded him to abandon opera. He survived because even his enemies recognized that he was arguably the century's greatest composer.

Dmitri Dmitrievich Shostakovich's career was marked by political and social unrest and controversy. Nevertheless, his musical output was consistently brilliant.

Shostakovich

A child prodigy, Dmitri Dmitrievich Shostakovich entered the Petrograd Conservatory in 1919 at the age of thirteen, studying under Alexander Glazunov. He came to public notice with his first symphony, written as his graduation piece in 1926. A taste of what was to follow, however, came in 1929 with the lukewarm official reception for his satirical opera, *Nos* (*The Nose*), which was criticized by the Composers' Union for its "formalism." As with so much of Shostakovich's music, the opera is a montage of different styles, ranging from popular songs and folk music to atonality.

Official condemnation

During the early 1930s, Shostakovich began work on his second opera, *Ledi Makbet Mtsenskovo Uyezda* (*Lady Macbeth of the Mtsensk District*). Based on a novella by Nikolai Leskov, it is set in 19th century Russia and is the story of a lonely provincial woman whose love for one of her husband's servants leads her into adultery, murder, and suicide. First staged in 1934, the opera was initially a great success. In the West, it was hailed as the first great Soviet opera. In 1936, however, when

A recent Mariinsky Theater production of Shostakovich's satirical opera *Nos* (*The Nose*), which was first performed in 1929 to indifferent reviews.

there were three productions of the opera running simutaneously in Moscow, an article entitled "Muddle Instead of Music" appeared in Pravda. Inspired, if not actually written, by Stalin, the article accused Shostakovich of "formalism" and the opera was withdrawn from performance. It was banned for almost thirty years, until a revised version, renamed *Katerina Ismailova*, was produced in 1962. It is now generally referred to by its original title.

On the lighter side

Shostakovich's music is often seen in the West as very somber and serious. Indeed, his greatest works, treading as they do a delicate path between the need to receive official approval and the desire to express his humanitarian ideals and his opposition to totalitariansim, have a feeling of tension and loneliness that few, if any, other composers have ever achieved. Despite this, however, Shostakovich also wrote a great deal of much lighter music, including his Jazz Suites, the numerous film scores and a musical comedy, *Moscow Cheremushki*.

must know

St. Petersburg—During the First World War the Russian variant of the city's name, Petrograd, was adopted. In 1924, it was renamed Leningrad, the name St. Petersburg being readopted in 1991.

British opera

After Purcell's *Dido and Aeneas* and Gay's *Beggar's Opera*, there was very little British opera until the 20th century, apart from the operettas of Gilbert and Sullivan. At the turn of the century, however, there were a number of composers who sought to produce operas in a specifically British style.

must know

Holst and Vaughan Williams—who were lifelong friends—became interested in old English folksongs, madrigal singers, and Tudor composers early in their musical careers. Holst shared Vaughan Williams' admiration for the simplicity and economy of these melodies, and their use in his compositions is one of his music's most recognizable features.

Holst

Gustav Holst (1874–1934) is best known for his orchestral suite, *The Planets*. His music was influenced by both English folk song and Indian mysticism. He wrote eight operas, including *Savitri* (1908), based on the Hindu epic the *Mahabharata*, and *The Perfect Fool* (1923), a one-act comic opera now best known for its ballet music. He drew on Shakespearean sources for *At the Boar's Head* (1923), which deals with the Falstaff scenes from Henry IV.

Gustav Holst wrote a number of operas with notably diverse themes and influences.

Vaughan Williams

Ralph Vaughan Williams (1872–1958) wrote nine symphonies as well as choral music and numerous film scores. One of these, for the film *Scott of the Antarctic*, formed the basis for his Seventh Symphony, *Sinfonia Antarctica*. He was a collector of British folk music and served as president of the English Folk Dance and Song Society. Vaughan Williams wrote five operas, including *Hugh the Drover* (1924) and *The Pilgrim's Progress*, which he worked on for nearly forty years. He also produced a Falstaff opera, *Sir John in Love* (1928).

Delius

Whereas Holst and Vaughan Williams drew largely on English folk music, Frederick Delius was influenced by Celtic themes. Born in Bradford in 1862, of German descent, he spent much of his life abroad, chiefly in the United States and France. In later life, Delius suffered from blindness and paralysis. His greatest works were all dictated to Eric Fenby, his amanuensis. Delius produced six operas, the best known of which is *A Village Romeo and Juliet* (1907). He died in 1934.

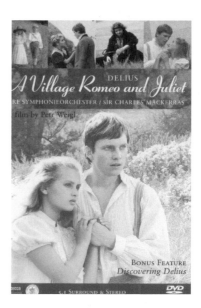

Benjamin Britten

The first British opera to win international recognition was Britten's *Peter Grimes* (1945). In the 1930s Britten had deliberately set himself apart from the English musical establishment, which he felt was complacent and inward-looking. He admired such European composers as Mahler, Stravinsky, and Berg, who were still regarded as dangerously modern in Britain.

An outsider's life

A native of Lowestoft in Suffolk, Britten was born in 1913. He began composing as a child, but his first compositions to attract attention were the Sinfonietta and the choral work *A Boy is Born* (1934). The following year, he met the poet W. H. Auden, with whom he collaborated on a number of compositions, while in 1936 he began his life-long relationship with the tenor, Peter Pears. In 1939, Britten and Pears, both pacifists, moved to the United States. It was there that Britten produced his first opera, *Paul Bunyan*, along with a number of orchestral works. They returned to England

Benjamin Britten was a self-styled outsider who prided himself on his musical and political unorthodoxy. His opera *Peter Grimes* remains part of the standard repertoire.

Peter Grimes is Britten's best-known opera. Its protagonist is a loner and misfit who is accused of murdering his young apprentice.

in 1942. Britten had his greatest success in 1945 with *Peter Grimes* but, by this time, he was experiencing opposition from various sections of the musical establishment, not only because of his music but also because of his politics and lifestyle. He withdrew to his Suffolk roots, founding the Aldeburgh Festival in 1948, partly to provide a showcase for his own works.

Britten's operas

Britten produced thirteen operas and "church parables." Many of these share common themes, particularly that of the "outsider." Such a character, misunderstood by society, is the protagonist of *Peter Grimes*, *Billy Budd* (1951), *Owen Wingrave* (1971), and *Death in Venice* (1973). These roles were all created with Peter Pears in mind. Another feature of Britten's operas is the presence of the sea, notably in *Peter Grimes*, which is actually set in Aldeburgh and includes the well-known orchestral "Sea Interludes." Britten died of heart failure in 1976. Despite the controversy surrounding his music and lifestyle, he had been made a life-peer in the same year and is now recognized as the major British composer of the 20th century.

must know

Like Britten, Michael Tippett was a controversial figure on the British musical scene. A left-wing homosexual and a conscientious objector in World War II, he was open to many different musical styles and his operas include elements of jazz and blues. His best-known, and most controversial, opera is *The Midsummer Marriage* (1955).

Peter Grimes

First performed in London on June 7th, 1945, Benjamin Britten's *Peter Grimes* is based on *The Borough*, a poem by George Crabbe. In the opera, however, the character of Grimes is not just a straightforward villain. As Britten put it, "The more brutal the society, the more brutal the individual."

Prologue

At an inquest, Peter Grimes, a fisherman, is questioned about the death of his apprentice. The townsfolk clearly think Grimes is guilty, although the coroner disagrees. Ellen Orford, the schoolmistress, tries to comfort Grimes, who rages against what he sees as the community's small-mindedness.

Peter Grimes is set on the Suffolk coastline where its composer, Benjamin Britten, spent most of his adult life.

Act I

When Grimes comes back from fishing, no one is willing
to give him a hand to pull his boat ashore except Captain
Balstrode and Ned Keene. Keene tells Grimes that he
has found another workhouse boy to be his apprentice.
Balstrode asks why Grimes does not move elsewhere,
but he answers that he intends to make money and
then marry Ellen. Grimes enters the pub and sits alone.
As a storm begins to rage, Ellen arrives with John, the
new apprentice. Grimes drags him away without even
a warm drink, to the disapproval of everyone.

Act II

As Ellen and John sit by the quay, some weeks later, she is
horrified to discover a bruise on his neck. Grimes comes
for the boy and says that he got the bruise accidentally.
They argue and he hits her. This exchange is observed by
the townspeople, who form a vigilante party to visit
Grimes in his hut. Hearing the approaching procession,
he gets ready to set out to sea and tells John to be careful
climbing down the cliff to his boat. John slips, however,
and falls to his death. When the mob reaches the hut,
Grimes is gone, and they find nothing out of order.

Act III

The busybody Mrs Sedley overhears a conversation
between Ellen and Balstrode. Grimes's boat is back
but there is no sign of the boy and the boy's jersey
has been found washed up on the shore. Armed with
this knowledge, the mob goes searching for Grimes.
Balstrode encourages him to take his boat out to sea
and sink it. The next morning, the town begins its
day anew. There is a report from the coast guard of
a boat sinking off the coast.

American opera

Immigrants from Italy, Germany, and France brought their own national styles of opera with them and, throughout the 19th century, European opera was dominant, though operas by American composers had appeared as early as the 18th century. A distinctive American style did not take hold until the 20th century.

Scott Joplin, pioneer of ragtime piano music. His music was immortalized when it was used in the 1970s film *The Sting*.

Ragtime and Jazz

Ragtime emerged as a style of piano playing around 1890 in the town of Sedalia, Missouri. It closely followed the form of European military marches, but while the left hand consisted of a regular "oom-pah" figure, the right-hand cut across this with syncopated melody lines. This became known as "ragged time," later shortened to "ragtime." The music was soon adapted to other instruments and small bands. It is difficult to say when ragtime evolved into jazz, but the pianist Jelly Roll Morton claimed that he *"invented jazz in 1902."* In *Black Music of Two Worlds* (1972), John Storm Roberts described jazz as *"perhaps the most important music of the 20th century."* It certainly has had a great influence on opera and other forms of musical theater in the United States.

Scott Joplin

Joplin was born in Texas in 1868. Unlike many other ragtime pianists, he wanted to be taken seriously as a composer. He insisted that his music be played exactly as written and particularly disliked the way in which so many ragtime pianists played everything quickly. Many of his rags were prefaced with the instruction "Not fast" or "Not

The notorious Cotton Club, in the heart of New York's Harlem, opened in 1923. Its "whites only" policy meant that all customers were caucasians, whereas all the performers at the club were black. It was the hub of the New York jazz scene for many years and attracted many top performers and much celebrity clientele. The club re-opened in 1978 and remains a shrine to jazz music to this day.

Cab Calloway performing at the Cotton Club. A forerunner of the club was opened in Harlem by the boxer Jack Johnson in 1920. Owney Madden took over in 1923, when the Cotton Club proper was born.

too fast." In 1911 he produced an opera, *Treemonisha*. Although often described as a "ragtime opera," it includes many other elements of African-American music, including blues and spirituals, as well as a call-and-response sequence between a congregation and a preacher. Its theme is the salvation of African-Americans through education, as its heroine, the teacher Treemonisha, confronts a local group of magicians. The opera was not performed in its entirety until 1970, when the full score was rediscovered. The score to an earlier opera by Joplin, *A Guest of Honor*, remains lost. Joplin wanted to experiment further with compositions like *Treemonisha*, but in 1916 his health worsened and he died in the Manhattan State Hospital in April, 1917.

George Gershwin

Jacob Gershowitz (George Gershwin) was the son of Russian Jewish parents. Born in New York in 1898, he wrote most of his vocal and theatrical works together with his elder brother and lyricist, Ira. Gershwin was

George Gershwin was an extremely gifted pianist as well as one of America's greatest and most popular composers.

a brilliant pianist with a natural gift for improvization. His songs were used extensively as a vehicle for improvization by jazz musicians and, in turn, he borrowed many ideas from jazz. He longed to be taken seriously as a composer, and when he met Ravel, Gershwin asked to become his student of composition. Ravel allegedly replied, *"Why should you be a second-rate Ravel when you can be a first-rate Gershwin?"* The opera *Porgy and Bess* was produced in 1935. Although it is set in an African-American community (and Gershwin demanded that it always be performed by an all-black cast) the opera also displays Gershwin's Jewish background, particularly the influence of *klezmer* music. Shortly afterward, Gershwin began to complain of blinding headaches. He had developed a brain tumor and died, during surgery, in 1937, at the age of only 38.

must know

Klezmer is a form of Jewish music developed initially in Eastern Europe. The klezmorim were itinerant musicians who played at weddings and other celebrations. They were often required to perform non-Jewish music, which they interpreted in their own style. The development of klezmer thus has much in common with jazz.

Musicals or opera?

While "serious" opera in the United States was generally based on European forms, light opera quickly developed a distinctive American style. Vaudeville, Yiddish theater, ragtime, and jazz all contributed to the unique form that became known as American Musical Theater, or more specifically, the Broadway Musical.

Broadway

Composers of musicals include Jerome Kern (1885–1945), Irving Berlin (1888–1989), Cole Porter (1891–1964), Richard Rogers (1902–1979), and Leonard Bernstein (1918–1990). The stories of their musicals are generally based on American themes, using predominantly American musical styles. They have much in common with the works of European nationalist composers of the 19th century and there are those who would argue that Broadway musicals are, in fact, American folk operas. The dividing line between operetta and musical is very blurred, especially when considering such musicals as Kern's *Showboat* (1927) or Bernstein's *West Side Story* (1957). In recent years, opera companies, especially in the United States, have begun to accord such musicals the recognition they deserve.

Recent Broadway productions of Kern's *Showboat* (below) and Bernstein's *West Side Story* (opposite).

Recent American opera

Composers who emigrated to the United States from the 1930s onward, as well as American born composers, have created operas in a distinctive American style, aware of alternatives to the traditional opera house and often concerning themselves with current events and issues.

Gian Carlo Menotti's broad and prolific output featured libretti that he personally produced in both Italian and English.

John Adams taught music for a number of years before producing several operas, including the notorious *The Death of Klinghoffer*.

Menotti

Gian Carlo Menotti, who was born in Cadegliano, Italy, in 1911, is the most famous and successful of America's émigré composers of opera. Following the death of his father, Menotti emigrated to the United States, where he enrolled in the Curtis Institute of Music in Philadelphia. His fellow students included Bernstein and Samuel Barber. Barber was to become Menotti's musical and life partner and Menotti wrote the libretto for Barber's opera *Vanessa* (1958). Menotti's first opera, *Amelia al Ballo* (*Amelia Goes to the Ball*) (1937) was written in Italian. His other operas, for all of which he wrote his own libretti, were in English. Following the success of *Amelia*, NBC commissioned an opera for radio, *The Old Maid and the Thief* (1939), the first such work ever written. This commission was followed in 1951 by *Amahl and the Night Visitors*, the first opera specifically composed for television. Among his other achievements were the verismo operas *The Medium*, *The Consul*, and *The Saint of Bleecker Street*, each of which was premiered on Broadway. He was also responsible for the creation of the Festival of the Two Worlds, an event held in Spoleto, Italy, since 1958, and, more recently, in Charleston, South Carolina. Menotti died in February 2006, aged 95.

John Adams

John Coolidge Adams, born in Massachusetts in 1947, graduated from Harvard in 1971. He taught at the San Francisco Conservatory of Music for ten years before being appointed as the contemporary music adviser and composer-in-residence of the San Francisco Symphony Orchestra. His opera *Nixon in China*, which was premiered in 1987, brought current affairs into the opera house and was followed, in 1991, by the more controversial opera *The Death of Klinghoffer*. This tells the story of the hijacking of the cruise-ship Achille Lauro in 1985 and the subsequent death of a Jewish-American passenger. *Doctor Atomic* (2005) deals with the creation of the atom bomb.

Philip Glass

The minimalist music of Philip Glass has made him one of the few composers of "art" music who have managed to also enjoy popular success. The son of Lithuanian Jewish parents, he was born in Baltimore in 1937. At the age of fifteen, he entered the University of Chicago, where he studied Mathematics and Philosophy, before enrolling at the Juilliard School of Music. This was followed by time in Paris, India, and Tibet, where he became a Buddhist. His first opera was *Einstein on the Beach* (1975), followed by *Satyagraha*, based on the early life of Mahatma Gandhi, in 1980. *Akhnaten* (1984), his first opera to use a full symphony orchestra, includes text in Biblical Hebrew and Ancient Egyptian. More recent operas include *Galileo Galilei* (2002) and *Waiting for the Barbarians* (2005), as well as numerous compositions for voices and chamber ensemble.

want to know more?

This chapter could only touch on some of the developments in 20th century music. To learn more, try:

- *20th-century Music: A History of Musical Style in Modern Europe and America* (Norton Introduction to Music History) by Robert P. Morgan, 1991)
- *Testimony: The Memoirs of Dmitri Shostakovich* by Solomon Volkov (Faber and Faber, 2005), gives an insight into the life of the composer.

Philip Glass is unusual in his opera celebrity insofar as much of his music is relatively inaccessible.

9 Stagecraft

So far we have been mainly concerned with the composers of operas and with their librettists. In this section, however, we will consider the great opera houses of the world, the actual staging of operas, and the roles of the stage designer and producer.

The great opera houses

The earliest operas were performed in palaces, but public opera houses were already being constructed in Italy as early as 1637, when the Teatro San Cassiano opened in Venice. In 1678, the first opera house outside Italy was built in Hamburg, followed by Paris and the other capitals of Europe.

La Scala

Perhaps the world's most famous opera house, the Teatro alla Scala in Milan, opened in August 1778 with a performance of *L'Europa Riconosciuta* by Antonio Salieri. It replaced an earlier theater, the Teatro Ducale, which was destroyed by fire in February 1776. The theater takes its name from the church of Santa Maria della Scala, which formerly occupied the site. Designed by Giuseppe Piermarini, it had over three thousand seats, arranged in six tiers of boxes. Funding was raised by selling *palchi* (private boxes) to wealthy citizens. These palchi were extravagantly decorated by their owners and La Scala became the place to be seen for Milanese high society. Following the tradition of the time, the *platea* (the main floor) had no seating and, until the *golfo mistico* (orchestra pit) was constructed in the 19th century, the orchestra was in full sight. La Scala was also a casino, with gamblers sitting in the foyer.

The Loggione

Above the tiers of boxes a gallery, the *loggione*, was constructed, where less wealthy patrons could watch performances. The loggione has always been crowded with the most critical of operagoers, who

The world famous La Scala opera house in Milan, Italy.

traditionally show their approval—or disapproval—very loudly. While good performances would be greeted with ecstatic applause from the *loggionisti*, inferior singers could expect boos, catcalls, and *fischi* (whistles of derision). Even today, there are two organizations for supporters of La Scala, Amici della Scala and Amici della Loggione.

Renovation

La Scala has been renovated several times during its history, most notably after World War II, when it had to be rebuilt after suffering extensive bomb damage. The theater was closed from 2002 until 2004 for an extensive modernization project. The stage was entirely reconstructed, with an enlarged backstage area, and improved seating arrangements now allow members of the audience to follow opera libretti on projected titles. The theater reopened in December 2004 with a performance of the same Salieri opera that was performed on its original opening night.

Paris

Famous as the setting for *The Phantom of the Opera*, Palais Garnier was the thirteenth theater to house the Paris Opera since it was founded in 1669. The building was often called the Paris Opera, but since the Opéra Bastille was built in 1989 as a second venue for Opéra National de Paris, the name Palais Garnier has been used.

Palais Garnier

The building was designed by Charles Garnier in 1861, and formed part of Baron Haussman's great reconstruction of Paris. Construction of the Palais Garnier was interrupted by the Franco-Prussian War (1870–1871) and the period of the Paris Commune (1871), as well as the difficulties of building on what was very marshy ground. The area of the Right Bank on which the building stands had always been very wet, and an underground lake situated beneath the site necessitated continous pumping for eight months before the foundations could finally be laid. Even after such drastic measures, the Parisian workmen continued to have difficulties.

The Palais Garnier eventually opened in January 1875, with a performance of Fromental Halévy's *La Juive* and excerpts from Meyerbeer's *Les Huguenots*. Viewed as one of the architectural masterpieces of the period, the theater is extremely ornate, with multi-colored marble decoration, velvet, gold-leaf, classical statuary, and a central chandelier weighing over six tons. The enormous stage has room for up to four hundred and fifty artists, enabling the biggest and most ambitious of opera productions to be staged with ease.

The opulent Palais Garnier stands at the very heart of Paris and is rightly regarded as one of the architectural triumphs of its era.

Bayreuth

Opened one year later than the Palais Garnier, the Bayreuth Festspielhaus (Bayreuth Festival Theater) could not be more different. Where the Palais Garnier is opulent, the Bayreuth theater is austere. Only the front entrance displays any ornamentation, while the remainder is mostly undecorated brick.

Wagner's theater

The most notable feature of the Festspielhaus is the orchestra pit, which is under the stage and covered by a hood. The orchestra is thus invisible to the audience. The design also alters the balance between singers and audience, with the mixed

The plain, brick red exterior of the Bayreuth Festspielhaus belies the consistently extraordinary events which go on inside.

sound of singers and orchestra being projected out into the enormous fan-shaped ampitheater. Another feature of the theater is the double proscenium, which makes the stage appear to be farther away than it is in reality. Wagner was particularly proud of this feature, referring to it as providing a "mystic gulf" between the audience and the stage.

The Bayreuth Festival

The Bayreuth Festspielhaus is the venue for the annual Bayreuth Festival, for which it was specifically conceived and built. Its construction, supervised by Wagner himself, was largely funded by King Ludwig II of Bavaria. It was first opened for the premiere of the complete four-opera cycle of *Der Ring des Nibelungen* (*The Ring of the Nibelungs*), in August 1876. This first Bayreuth Festival was attended by the Emperor of Germany, the Emperor and Empress of Brazil, the King of Bavaria, Prince George of Prussia, Grand Duke Vladimir of Russia, and a host of lesser nobility. Some sixty newspapers from all over the world sent reporters, those from the *New York Times* and *Tribune* using the new transatlantic telegraph cable to get their stories through quickly. The correspondent from the London *Times* complained that *"the great distance from the town over a dirty road with no shade and no restaurant accommodation caused much discontent."*

Bayreuth's history has been checkered, with the town and festival becoming a focus of Nazi ideology during World War II. Nazi leaders would regularly patronize the festival, until it closed when the town was heavily bombed toward the end of the war, re-opening once more in 1951.

must know

Today the Bayreuth Festival is as popular an event as it was when it first took place in 1876. Tens of thousands of people attend the festival each year and it has been sold out annually without fail since its inception. Currently, waiting lists for tickets can stretch for up to 10 years or more.

London

The Royal Opera House is the third theater on the site in Covent Garden. The first Theatre Royal, as it was originally called, was opened in December 1732 by the actor and theater manager John Rich, who had become wealthy following the success of John Gay's *Beggar's Opera*, which he had commissioned.

Covent Garden

For the first hundred years of its life, the theater was mainly a playhouse, though the operas of Handel were performed there, and were indeed the first serious musical works to be heard at Covent Garden. This original theater was destroyed by fire in 1808 and was rebuilt in the following year. At the time, Her Majesty's Theatre in the Haymarket was the principal venue for opera in London. In 1846, however, Michael Costa, the conductor at Her Majesty's, moved to Covent Garden. The auditorium was redesigned and the theater was renamed the Royal Italian Opera, opening in April 1847 with a performance of Rossini's *Semiramide*. In 1856, the theater

London's Royal Opera House is situated in Covent Garden at the heart of the city and is surrounded by buildings of many different vintages.

was burned down yet again. The present theater opened in 1858, with a performance of Meyerbeer's *Les Huguenots*. In 1892, the theater was renamed as The Royal Opera House.

The Royal Opera Company

During World War II, the theater in Covent Garden became a dance hall, but in 1946 it reopened as an opera house, with its own resident company, the Covent Garden Opera. The original plan was to present operas only in English, but this policy was later abandoned. In October 1968, the Queen granted the company the right to be called The Royal Opera. In 1995, work began on major reconstruction of the opera house. This entailed the demolition of almost the entire theater, apart from the auditorium, and made the Royal Opera House arguably the most modern opera venue in Europe.

New York

The Academy of Music was built in New York in 1854 for the presentation of opera. It was patronized by New Yorks's upper crust, who were reluctant to admit new members to their exclusive society.

The Met

The Metropolitan Opera Association was founded in 1880 as an alternative, its initial group of subscribers including members of the Morgan, Roosevelt, Vanderbilt, and Astor families. The Metropolitan Opera House opened in October 1883 with a performance of Gounod's *Faust*. The auditorium contained 122 boxes, to accommodate the city's growing population of millionaires (the Academy only had eighteen). The opera was a place to be seen and more attention was paid to the design of the auditorium than the stage, which was very cramped. This meant that productions were rather static, though the wealth of the board members ensured that the world's most famous singers could be engaged. In the early years, company policy toward language changed several times. At first, everything was performed in Italian and later everything was in German. Finally, it was decided that operas should be performed in their original language.

The move to Lincoln Center

Following a fire in 1892, the building was extensively renovated but was still felt to be too small. A much larger audience, however, was reached by the Met's famous radio broadcasts, which started on

The somewhat futuristic 1960s design of the Metropolitan Opera House at New York's Lincoln Center divides critics and has attracted controversy.

Christmas Day 1931 with a performance of Humperdinck's *Hansel und Gretel* and which still continue more than seven decades later. There were numerous plans to move to larger premises, but it was not until 1966 that the Metropolitan Opera moved to its present location at Lincoln Center. The original building was demolished in 1967. The new Metropolitan Opera House (pictured on page 170), which has a seating capacity of four thousand, opened in September 1966 with the world premiere of Samuel Barber's *Antony and Cleopatra*.

Five famous designers

Stage spectacle has always formed an important part of opera. Nowadays, opera companies often perform works that have become familiar through being in the repertoire for so long. Opera also faces competition from film, television, and other media. The role of the director has thus become ever more important.

The Italian director Franco Zeffirelli, pictured with the star of his famous film production of *Romeo and Juliet*, Olivia Hussey.

Franco Zeffirelli

Franco Zeffirelli (born Gianfranco Corsi in 1923) is best known as a film director, especially for his lavish interpretation of Shakespeare's *Romeo and Juliet*, for which he won an Academy Award in 1968. Since the 1950s, however, he has also been a major director of opera productions, working at Covent Garden (*Tosca*, *Rigoletto*), the New York Metropolitan Opera (*Don Giovanni*, *Otello*, *Tosca*, *Turandot*), the Paris Opera (*Norma*, *La Traviata*), and La Scala (*La Bohème*, *Cavalleria Rusticana*, *Pagliacci*, and *Turandot*).

In his long and distinguished career, Zeffirelli has also made several films of operas, including *La Traviata* (1982) and *Otello* (1986). His recent film, *Callas Forever*, is dedicated to the final years in the life of the Greek soprano, with whom he worked on numerous occasions.

After World War II, when he fought as a partisan, Zeffirelli studied art and architecture at the University of Florence, before going on to work with Italian film directors such as Roberto Rossellini and Luchino Visconti. This is reflected in his opera productions, which are noted for their scale and lavish designs.

Something of a contemporary Universal Man, Jonathan Miller is well known in several fields, not least that of international opera.

Jonathan Miller

Born in London in 1934, Jonathan Miller has become famous in numerous fields. Trained as a doctor of medicine, he was one of the members of the Cambridge Footlights Revue, who changed the course of British comedy in the early 1960s with the revue *Beyond the Fringe*. He wrote for the British satirical magazine *Private Eye* and presented the BBC's prestigious arts program *Monitor*. In 1966, he wrote and directed a notorious television adaptation of *Alice in Wonderland*. It was not until the 1970s that he started producing and directing operas, working first with Kent Opera and at Glyndebourne and then producing *The Marriage of Figaro* for the English National Opera in 1978. His productions are often controversial, particularly his Mafia-style *Rigoletto* for the English National Opera and his Royal Opera production of *Cosi Fan Tutte*, which had the cast dressed in designer clothes. He has also worked with the New York Metropolitan Opera and at La Scala.

Frank Corsaro

Frank Corsaro was born in New York City in 1924 and developed an early interest in theater. He started his professional life as an actor, working off Broadway and on television and radio, later turning to directing rather than acting. He directed his first opera in 1957, with his production of Carlisle Floyd's *Susannah*. It was another ten years before he returned to opera, with Shostakovich's *Katerina Ismailova*. Since then, he has worked with almost every major opera company in the United States, directing most of the operas from the standard repertory as well as numerous world premieres. He has also written several books about opera, including *Maverick: A Director's Personal Experience in Opera and Theater*.

Sarah Caldwell

Sarah Caldwell became the first female conductor of the New York Metropolitan Opera in 1976. Born in Maryville, Missouri, in 1924, she was a child prodigy and was giving public performances on the violin by the age of ten. She later attended the University of Arkansas and the New England Conservatory of Music. She produced her first opera, Vaughan Williams' *Riders to the Sea*, in 1947. In 1952 she became head of the Boston University opera workshop then founded the Opera Company of Boston in 1957. Here she made her name for directing difficult works, including the American premiere of Berlioz's *Les Troyens*, and arranging unusual variations of operas in the standard repertory. In a 1965 interview she had this to say about opera *"[It] is everything rolled into one—music,*

Sarah Caldwell was for half a century one of the most influential women working in opera until her retirement in 2004.

theater, the dance, color and voices, and theatrical illusions. Once in a while, when everything is just right, there is a moment of magic. People can live on moments of magic." She retired in 2004, due to poor health, and died of heart failure in March, 2006.

Peter Sellars

Peter Sellars was born in Pittsburgh, Pennsylvania in 1957. He attended Harvard University, where he once performed a puppet version of Wagner's *Ring Cycle*. He also directed a performance of Shakespeare's *Antony and Cleopatra* that took place in a swimming pool and one of *King Lear* that featured a Lincoln Continental onstage. In his senior year, a production of Handel's *Orlando* brought him to national attention. Sellars gained a reputation for his modern stagings of operas. These included Mozart's *Cosi Fan Tutte*, set in a Cape Cod diner, and *Don Giovanni*, set in Spanish Harlem. As his productions became known outside the United States, Sellars was invited to work at both the Salzburg and Glyndebourne Festivals, producing 20th century operas such as Messiaen's *François d'Assise*, Hindemith's *Mathis der Maler*, and Ligeti's *Le Grand Macabre*. He also directed the premieres of Adams' *Nixon in China* and *The Death of Klinghoffer*. He recently directed another Adams opera, *Dr Atomic*, about the development of the atomic bomb, for the San Francisco Opera, premiered to coincide with the sixtieth anniversary of the first nuclear bomb test. In 1998, Sellars was awarded the Erasmus Prize by the Dutch Praemium Erasmianum Foundation, for his contributions to European culture.

The American director Peter Sellars is renowned for his offbeat and highly imaginative opera productions.

want to know more?

The following books will give a further insight into the complexities of staging opera:

- *The Toughest Show on Earth: My Rise and Reign at the Metropolitan Opera by Joseph Volpe* (Alfred A. Knopf, 2006)
- *Valery Gergiev and the Kirov: A Story of Survival by John Ardoin* (Amadeus Press, 2003)

Need to know more?

If you are interested in exploring the world of opera in greater depth, there is a wide range of different resources available. The following selection of options includes a brief listing of performances on DVD of the operas featured in this book, useful websites, and recommendations for magazines and other books on the subject.

Opera on DVD

The following is a selection of currently available DVD recordings of the operas featured on colored pages in this book.

Aïda

Deutsche Grammophon—0730019
Starring Aprile Milo, Placido Domingo, and Dolora Zajick, this Metropolitan Opera production is conducted by James Levine and directed by Brian Large.
NVC Arts (Warner Music)—0630193892
A spectacular production recorded at the Arena di Verona in 1981, featuring Maria Chiara as Aïda and Fiorenza Cossotto as her rival, Amneris.

Boris Godunov

NVC Arts (Warner Music)—5101118512
A traditional Russian production recorded in 1987 at the Bolshoi Theatre in Moscow. The title role is sung by Evgeny Nesterenko and the conductor is Alexander Lazarev.
Philips—075 089-9
A BBC/Royal Opera House co-production,

with the orchestra and chorus of the Kirov Opera conducted by Valery Gergiev. It was directed for television by Humphrey Burton.

Carmen

Deutsche Grammophon—0730009
Starring Agnes Baltsa and José Carreras, this is another Metropolitan Opera production conducted by James Levine and directed by Brian Large.
Columbia Tristar—CDR10530
This is the Francesco Rosi film version, featuring Julia Migenes and Plácido Domingo.

Die Zauberflöte (The Magic Flute)

Deutsche Grammophon—0730039
This is the 1991 Metropolitan Opera production, with sets designed by David Hockney. It features Kathleen Battle, Francisco Araiza and Kurt Moll. The Metropolitan Opera Orchestra is conducted by James Levine.
Opus Arte Media Productions—OA0885D
A 2003 Royal Opera House television production directed by Sue Judd. It stars Willi Hartmann, Dorothea Röschmann, and

Diana Damrau. The Royal Opera House Orchestra is conducted by Colin Davis.

Faust

Deutsche Grammophon—0734108
The Vienna State Opera in a 1985 production by the film director Ken Russell.
Hardy Classic Video—HCD 4005
This is a 1987 production at Teatro Regio di Parma, with Alfredo Kraus in the title role and the Bulgarian bass, Nicola Ghiuselev as Méphistophélès.

Fidelio

Deutsche Grammophon—0730529
The Metropolitan Opera Orchestra and Chorus are conducted by James Levine in this 2000 production featuring Karita Mattila, Ben Heppner and René Pape.
Arthaus Musik—101099
This production, directed by Peter Hall, is from the 1979 Glyndebourne Festival. Bernard Haitink conducts the London Philharmonic Orchestra, with Elisabeth Soderstrom and Robert Allman.

Il Barbiere di Siviglia (The Barber of Seville)

NVC Arts (Warner Music)—4509992232
John Cox's 1982 Glyndebourne production was a great success with the critics.
Arthaus Musik—100090
The Cologne City Opera Choir and the

Stuttgart Radio Symphony Orchestra, with Cecilia Bartoli as Rosina and Gino Quilico as Figaro, in a 1988 production.

Madame Butterfly

Film version (2002) Sony B00005U0HI (Region 2); B00005UVDM (Region 1)
Featuring: Ying Huang, Richard Troxell, Ning Liang, Richard Cowan, Jing Ma Fan.
Madama Butterfly (2005), Deutsche Grammophon—B0007P0LO8
Featuring: Mirella Freni, Plácido Domingo, Christa Ludwig, Robert Kerns, Michel Sénéchal.

Peter Grimes

Opus Arte Media Productions—OA0885D
Elijah Moshinsky directs this Royal Opera House performance, starring Norman Bailey and Heather Harper.
Arthaus Musik—100382
This is a BBC recording from 1994, featuring the English National Opera Orchestra and Chorus, with Philip Langridge as Peter Grimes and Janice Cairns as Ellen Orford.

Tristan und Isolde

Deutsche Grammophon—0730449
A Metropolitan Opera production, with Ben Heppner and Jane Eaglen. James Levine conducts.
Opus Arte—OA0935D
John Treleaven and Deborah Polaski take

the lead in this performance, with the Chorus and Symphony Orchestra of Barcelona's Gran Teatre del Liceu.

Wozzeck

Arthaus Musik—100256
The Vienna State Opera, conducted by Claudio Abbado, feature in this 1987 production directed by Brian Large.
Kultur—2915
Dale Duesing sings the title role in Peter Mussbach's production, with The Frankfurter Museum Orchestra and the Choir of the Frankfurter Opera.

Opera websites

www.operamania.com (Everything you might need to know about opera, available in several languages.)
www.AllAboutOpera.com (As the name suggests—a general site, all about opera.)
www.geocities.com/Vienna/7023/ (A comprehensive guide to opera recordings, both audio and video.)
www.metmaniac.com/ (An independent site dedicated to the Metropolitan Opera's radio and television broadcasts.)
www.usoperaweb.com/ (An online magazine dedicated to American opera.)
www.operatoday.com/ (Online magazine devoted to all aspects of opera.)
www.operabase.com (Publishes opera information in 27 different languages.)

www.metoperafamily.org/metopera/ home (Metropolitan Opera website.)
www.sfopera.com (San Francisco Opera website.)
www.royalopera.org (Royal Opera House website.)
www.operastuff.com (Provides links to hundreds of other opera websites with a multitude of different information.)

Opera magazines

BBC Music Magazine (musicmagazine@originpublishing.co.uk)
The Gramophone (www.gramophone.co.uk)
Opera (www.opera.co.uk)
Opera News (www.metoperafamily.org/operanews)
Opera Now (www.rhinegold.co.uk/ magazines/on)

Further reading

Boyden, Matthew, *The Rough Guide to Opera* (Rough Guides, 1999)
Forman, Sir Denis, *The Good Opera Guide* (Weidenfeld & Nicolson, 2001)
Holden, Amanda (Ed.), *The New Penguin Opera Guide* (Penguin, 2001)
Parker, Roger (Ed.), *The Oxford Illustrated History of Opera* (Oxford University Press)
Plotkin, Fred, *Opera 101—A Complete Guide to Learning and Loving Opera* (Hyperion, 1994)

Index

Acknowledgments

The publishers would like to thank the following companies and individuals for supplying images for inclusion in this book: **Redferns:** 175, 179, 181 (credit: Arcaid); 158 (credit: David Farrell); 184(T) (credit: www.hawaiiopera.org);2, 80, 90, 147(T&B),(credit: Henrietta Butler); 154 (credit: Hunstein/RSC); 170 (credit: Grossman/RSC); 183 (credit: imageartists.com/Malcolm MacLaren); 164 (credit: Max Jones Files); 151, 162, 163; (credit: Michael Ochs Archive); 167 (credit: Nicky J. Sims); 10, 18, 28, 54, 69, 71, 73, 83, 94, 100, 104, 110, 118, 146, 165; (credit: Palm/RSCH); 93, 119, 125(B) (credit: Phil Dent); 40, 51, 60, 64, 65, 66, 72, 75, 76, 77, 87, 91, 99, 103, 106, 115, 120, 125(T), 126(T&B), 129, 134, 137, 138, 139(T&B), 140, 141, 143, 145, 159, 160, 168 (credit: Ron Scherl); 185 (credit: sfopera.com); 46, 55, 56(B), 63, 70, 85, 98, 108, 136, 142, 152 (credit: The Bridgeman Art Library); **Others:** www.arnolddrawls.com: 7; www.banffcentre.ca: 49; www.bmgnews: 6; www.columbia.edu: 97(B); www.cs.princeton.edu: 114; www.festivalmozart.com: 15; www.imgartists.com: 111; www.losangelesopera.com: 78, 79; www.metronimo.com: 53, 56(T), 57; stuarthowe.com: 116; www.telegraph.co.uk: 26; www.wilander.com: 47.

Key: T= Top; B = Bottom; L = Left; R = Right